I0560493

WILD JOY

**Ecospiritual Encounters
with Nature as Teacher,
Healer, and Lover**

PRAISE FOR *WILD JOY*

This is how you teach us, Larry, with kindness for all that we carry, even the hard-to-hold parts, the parts that cast shadows and yet belong to the wild whole.

—Nell Devito, Educator in Leadership and Human Development, Bio-Leadership Fellow, ICF Master Certified Coach, Nature Guide Colleague

The religious and home environment Larry and I grew up in was an immersion in confusing messages about an angry but "loving God" from a passionate evangelical preacher who was also our authoritarian and abusive father and provider. Larry's path, as the family scapegoat and as one with a propensity for asking forbidden questions, was to choose a courageous life of personal authenticity, self-discovery, and genuine truth-seeking over the comforts of inherited answers, community, and familiarity.

Wild Joy reveals the challenges and struggles of what it can be to confront and transform a worldview and "self" that are not in coherence with the landscape of our habitation. His storytelling and adventures invite and inspire the reader into a willingness to explore the same within themselves.

—Benny Glover, Retired-Licensed Marriage and Family Therapist, Psychotherapist

What makes this book especially powerful is how it weaves together an ecological perspective on healing with the wisdom of the outdoors and a profound spiritual openness. **Wild Joy** *is a must-read for anyone seeking personal liberation and a deeper connection to life.*

—Karin Lubin, EdD, Life Coach
Author of *My Life Through the Seasons: A Wisdom Journal and Planner* series, Co-author of *The Conscious Journal to Self-Love* and *Living From My Centered Self: An IFS Wisdom Journal, Calmness and Confidence*

Born into a parentage that had all the prescribed answers and formulas for their offspring, a so-called fundamentalism that meted out harsh spiritual, physical, and emotional retributions, Larry Glover grew up amidst the cruel irony of those saving souls by crushing them. In **Wild Joy***, he shares from decades of gripping and magical encounters with spirit animals and plants that become his guides and foundation for his most powerful work in the world, learning to bring love home to self and to a world seduced into self-destruction by a theology of superiority and separation.*

Far more than one man's journey out of painful separation from self and soul, Larry Glover's life story helps me ponder both my own trials along the path to a fuller humanhood and our entire society's struggle to grow up by replacing domination over nature with authentic connection to our precious Earth as "healer, teacher and lover."

—Randy Crutcher, EdD, Pioneer in the Awakening Men's Movement, Co-author of *The Passion Principle, How to Live YOUR Most Passionate Life*

In an age of increasing disconnection from both nature and each other, this remarkable book reminds us that our deepest healing often lies in reclaiming our place within the web of life and the cosmos. Larry Glover's journey out of an oppressive fundamentalism into a life of ecological communion, set against the backdrop of America's most transformative cultural decades, offers a hopeful blueprint for personal transformation precisely when such visions are most needed.
—Carlos Gonzales, PhD, Clinical Psychologist

Wild Joy *is an invitation to rediscover the healing power of nature for those carrying the invisible wounds of personal trauma. Through heartfelt storytelling and profound transparency, this book gently guides readers on a journey from pain to wholeness, offering solace and inspiration to discover the profound ways nature as teacher can help us heal and transform.*

With each page, the author's compassion and authenticity shine through, creating a sense of companionship and encouragement—like sitting down with a trusted friend who truly understands the depths of sorrow and the heights of hope. The stories and reflections are not only deeply moving but also universally relatable, reminding us that we are never alone in our struggles or our longing for joy and interconnection.

Wild Joy *is a gift for the heart, a balm for the spirit, and a testament to the enduring power of nature to heal, uplift, and restore life.*
—Rochelle Calvert, PhD, Author of *Healing with Nature: Mindfulness and Somatic Practices to Heal from Trauma*

WILD JOY

**Ecospiritual Encounters
with Nature as Teacher,
Healer, and Lover**

LARRY GLOVER

Copyright © 2025 Larry Glover
All rights reserved. No part of this book may be used or reproduced in any manner without written permission from the author and publisher, except by reviewers, bloggers, or other individuals who may quote brief passages, as long as they are clearly credited to the author.

Neither the publisher nor the author is engaged in rendering professional advice or services to the individual reader. The ideas and suggestions contained in this book are not intended as a substitute for professional help. Neither the author nor the publisher shall be liable or responsible for any loss or damage allegedly arising from any information or suggestion in this book.

Scripture taken from the New King James Version®. Copyright © 1982 by Thomas Nelson. Used by permission. All rights reserved.

Seshat Press
211 Pauline Drive #513
York, PA 17402
www.seshatpress.com
Send questions to: support@seshatpress.com

Paperback ISBN: 979-8-9920502-5-7
eBook ISBN: 979-8-9920502-6-4
Library of Congress Control Number: 2025909664

Cover Design: Ranilo Cabo
Layout: Ranilo Cabo
Editor and Proofreader: Simon Whaley
Book Midwife: Karen Everitt

Printed in the United States of America

Seshat Press is proud to be a part of the Tree Neutral® program. Tree Neutral offsets the number of trees consumed in the production and printing of this book by taking proactive steps such as planting trees in direct proportion to the number of trees used to print books. To learn more about Tree Neutral, please visit treeneutral.com.

DISCLAIMER

As reflected in this book, the soul medicine of psychedelic mushrooms is integral to my journey of discovering nature as a healer, teacher, and lover. As also reflected here, psychedelics are not to be lightly engaged with. Their potential gifts are many, including *expanded states of consciousness* and an increased sense of belonging and connectivity. But along the way, they will also likely challenge and even dismantle your constructed sense of identity. *Bad trips* are always possible, especially when the entheogen is not partaken of with proper respect, intention, set, setting, and dosage awareness. My story is a testimony to the possible dangers and fortunes of surviving self-initiation experimentation without formal mentorship.

Yes, at lower doses, they can also have recreational value. However, the greater awareness and respect one comes to them with, the greater transformational, supportive, and nurturing value they will bring to your soul and spirit. When engaged in this spirit, as sentient beings of themselves, they can indeed be soul medicine for our times.

The underlying message here is if you choose to partake of, get educated. Differences between recreational, clinical, and self or group initiation and medicine experiences can be vast. Today's available resources are rich and growing, despite the continuing illegalities. Beware of aspiring yet naïve teachers and pseudo-gurus. See the Resources links on the author's webpage for a sampling of trusted resources.

Neither the author nor the publisher intend for any content in this book to be a recommendation for your usage of psychedelics. Nor do either assume any responsibility or liability for your usage.

To the wild joy and feral resiliency living within each of us, calling us home to ourselves as Source and co-creators of the deep Self we are.

To Mother Sophia, Gaia, Earth, the sacred feminine living within all that is.

To all children who will inherit the world we leave you.

To Bear for saving my life, time and again, in my loneliest hours of need.

To the great unspeakable mystery, for this I Am—of existence, for the gifts of conscious presence and breath, for the transformational gifts of curiosity, wonder, awe, and gratitude.

AUTHOR'S NOTE

The stories I share here are intimately mine, as are the inherent biases and perspectives.

I intend these perspectives as no judgment, degradation, or demeaning of the beliefs of others, though the reader will quickly note my story soon becomes that of self-righteous, rage-filled youth and heretic. Our times are, however, in-between story times, when old worldviews fight vigorously for their lives while a new story of sacred kinship, though itself of ancient antiquity, is re-birthing itself anew.

Such cycles of death and rebirth require initiations of our souls and spirits, and reconfigurations, even of our essential identity. Wherever you may be on this journey, I bow to you and your path, even as I continue to learn to bow to my own.

In appreciation, honor, and respect for fellow companions along this journey, and to protect their anonymity, I have changed names and minimized certain location identifiers.

CONTENTS

FOREWORD

"I'm not like other people," Larry tells me the first time we meet. "I don't live in the same world most folks do."

We're at a Wilderness First Aid course in Santa Fe. I'd heard Larry's name through friends when I first moved to town and began looking for a new collaborator for the wilderness programs I led. As I read through his website, I thought he'd be a perfect partner—someone who brought so much deep experience with and knowledge of the natural world, not just from an ecological perspective but from a spiritual one as well. But that depth made me nervous too—what would he think of me, in some ways, his opposite: an Ivy-educated, East-coast atheist with an MBA who until now had lived in cities her whole life, run a research consulting company and lived smack in the middle of American culture with a husband, two kids, and a cat? My heart was beginning to open to the power of nature though, and the draw of learning to see nature as a teacher, healer, and lover, as Larry likes to say, luckily outweighed my inner anxieties.

Nearly fifteen years later, having created countless programs in nature together, I look back at this serendipitous encounter with gratitude and awe. That's also how I've felt witnessing the many transformations among the people we've worked with—what an incredible honor. It's also how I feel about this memoir. In it, Larry shares his healing journey from growing up in an abusive ultra-religious home, to fighting forest fires as a young man questioning received wisdom on all fronts, and creating such a deeply meaningful relationship with nature that it saved his life again and again.

Larry's story is one to which we can all relate, no matter how different the details of our lives. It asks us to look at how we're living—and also how we're facing death—as he explores how the two are innately and intimately connected. It asks us to listen—to the trees, to the rivers, to each other, but most importantly to our own hearts, and to not be led astray by our domineering heads. It asks us to love because, at its core, this is a love story—of a man learning to love himself, by seeing himself as one with nature. With this memoir, Larry has done the hard work for us, weaving stories and poems into a beautiful work of art that took over forty years and plumbed the depth of his soul. Thank you, Larry. The world is a better place because of you and this book.

Cheryl Slover-Linett
Companion for Self-discovery through Nature
Author of *Seduction of the Daughter in Fifteen Pieces*
Leadfeather.org

INTRODUCTION

The Kingdom of the Father is spread out upon the earth, and people do not see it.

—Gospel of Thomas (Saying 113)

—Elaine Pagels

Beyond Belief: The Secret Gospel of Thomas

There are two paths I have followed into the wild explorations of what it is to be human. One is the inherited path of domestication into fear, self-denial, domination, and subjugation to externalized power structures of control. The other is the wild game trail, or mystically ascribed *left-hand path*, the feral path of full-hearted self-acceptance and love, and forbidden transformational birthrights I discovered that lie already living within, awaiting my embrace.

Wandering these paths, in search of truth, freedom, and bearings for my lost soul, in search of understanding and conscious authorship of a life of my creation and choosing, are the tales of my living. They are the tales of release and letting go of worldview stories and patterns that no longer serve. These are the tales of stumbling past the proverbial and Biblical guardians at the garden gate. And so, they are also the tales of discovering the forbidden fruits of the Tree of Life as the antidote to the spiritual wounds intrinsic within the original heresy: a story of separation, domination, and control that denies our inherent sacred kinship with all that is.

The entheogenic soul medicine of psychedelic mushrooms is integral to my journey of discovering nature as a sacred healer, teacher, and lover. The invitation of incarnation I am learning to embody from this path is:

One Body

    One Spirit

        One Womb

            One Earth

                Celebrating Diversity.

For the Children

I am a man of story
And I wonder if I might be so presumptive
as to introduce myself

For you see, I am a lover of stories
and of poetry and all things beautiful
Like the Common Raven now croaking in the distance

Or the Tassel-eared squirrel that chirped Hello
but moments ago
Or Spring's white-spotted tan fawn

that curiously-cautiously rises from hiding
behind the large log lying in thick Gambles Oak
and for a moment thinks to sneak away

But when the three nearby Muley women folk
choose curiosity in response to my sweet talk
with ears intent on listening
their eyes deep and wild as a starless night

well my heart just spills open
And we talk
with tender love for the young ones

and all things living
including the silence so deep
you can hear the stars sing

or a Ponderosa pinecone drop onto the forest floor
and so give itself back to the ancestors and seed the future too
Oh but these are not the stories I thought to tell

Nevertheless I think indeed
here already I strip myself naked
before the eyes of your soul

Idolatry Re-Conceived

Listen to me
at risk of your own

for I am a man of contradictions
riddled with holy rage

pierced by wild grief and sorrow
yet full of a peace within

that flows in the same riverbed as gratitude and love.
Yet I yearn and long to be heard and seen and

crave I also to hide, shy as I am.
Inside the nearest tree will nicely do

where I feel more at home
than in any church of god

conceived by men yet asleep to their deep identity
and so serve beckoning shadows unseen

Chapter 1

SEEKING GOD ON A MOUNTAINTOP

I call it The Jehovah Wound. This grief, loneliness, and deprivation of soul and spirit that yet seeks to claim my life at times. It is the voice inside my head that tells me *I am not good enough. Never will be.*

This voice of self-denigration drives me to go alone to a remote Forest Service mountain-top fire lookout for three months of isolation. It is 1983. I'm thirty-four years old and this is my seventh season with the Forest Service. I typically hire on early spring for trail crew work, then transition to initial attack for fires once that season starts. My seasonal employment closes in the Fall with burning brush piles for fire prevention work. But there is a wildfire burning in my spirit and soul that requires attention from me.

My spiritual intention is to strike a killing blow to the God of my youth. I also aspire to write about, to better understand, and to deepen the journey of healing I have stumbled into. For though I am now blessed in uncountable ways, for Nature is unfolding as a sacred healer, teacher, and lover, I am yet a haunted man. Truth is, the childhood shadows of shame and unworthiness-for-living periodically insert their viral and spectral presence into the womb of my living.

There is also a promise to keep to the suicidal fifteen-year-old me—the one who ran away from home. In desperation, I surrendered and devoted my life to the Lord Jehovah God. Yet he is the one I now dream of saving the world from. My love of nature now nurtures the love of Life within, and I seek to honor Bear, who through a nose-to-nostril meeting in the doorway of my tent, in my early twenties, changed my world by changing my story, and so saved my life. Time and again. Still.

I also desire to share the transformational blessings that, a few years earlier, were gifted when I walked alone into the remote wilds of Idaho, to either die or to come out a different man, one reborn anew.

So, like Moses of old, I imagine, seeking freedom for his people from bondage in Egypt, it is both desperation and aspiration that bring me to this Fire Lookout. For I aspire, it is here I will fulfill my adolescent dreams of writing a book that will change the world. I will at last be revealed as the hero my suicidal nine-year-old imagined he might be, rather than the outcast and embarrassment to parents and God that I am.

I might as well begin with this wild story of how it is, on this mountain. I aim to look into the eyes of God and discover the truth of his being. For I desire freedom.

However, I don't know what to do with the story about freedom-seeking that my friend and crew boss, Dave, shares on our short helicopter ride up to the fire lookout from the Krassel Ranger Station.

"Have you heard the story of the guy we thought committed suicide up at the lookout?" Dave asks over the ship's radio, on our flight to the lookout.

"Uh, no, Dave. Tell me."

"Well, he'd call in for his daily radio check for a couple of weeks, saying he was losing it and had to come down. It was a busy year. And we needed him there. Then we didn't hear from him for a couple of days. So, we fly up and we see this body hanging from the rafters. Of course, we land. Then the guy comes running out of the lookout with his bags packed!"

Dave explains through his laughter, "He'd made a dummy and dressed it up, and it was a good one. Sure gave us a scare!"

This is a weird story to tell me, Dave, I think. *Especially just as I'm heading up to the lookout for my own three months of isolation. Like I don't have some burning in my stomach, along with excitement. I suspect he might be a bit hurt or insulted, though, that I'm leaving the crew. It's a bit like I'm blowing off a career path he's on as I take a downgrade in pay for this lookout job. I don't know...*

I've been around long enough though, to know Fire Lookouts, like us backcountry firefighters, are a breed of our own.

But here I am, once again, destined to be an outsider, walking away from a community where I've gained respect and some sense of belonging. And I notice too, the irony and humor of the United States Government supporting me on my intimate spiritual quest. Of course, they have no idea of the madness that drives me to the lookout that I struggle with inside.

This madness leaves me feeling alone in the world of men and drives two realizations. One is that the bureaucracy of the Forest Service will never be suitable for me to get any higher in the organization than these 6,842 feet of elevation at the lookout.

Secondly, and more importantly, I'd come with excitement into the Forest Service, believing that, for a change, I'd only be doing good, along with Smokey Bear, putting out fires and working in the wilds of nature. Only with the soles of my handmade White's firefighter boots on the ground, worth a month's pay, however, do I come to experience the trauma in our western forests caused by putting out all the wildfires we could for the last one hundred-plus years.

It's like I keep trying to do good in the world, saving souls for God first, then saving runaway kids from street life in the inner city of Detroit, then saving forests from wildfires, only to discover the good I intend is more wrapped up in ambiguities and paradoxes than my black and white map of reality allows. Now, however, my childhood hero, Smokey Bear, is no more to be trusted than parents, God, or the government. The world seems full of deception and lies. I crave Truth! And Freedom!

The helicopter's roar and sight slide into the distance as silence and stillness descend like mana from heaven. *This is what I've been waiting for!*

Before me stands a small, shuttered, white one-room twelve-foot by twelve-foot minimalist wooden haven, or potential hell, apparently. At my feet lies a backpack of personal gear, a few boxes of food and liquor, enough for a couple of weeks, a large box of books, and the high school graduation gift of a typewriter from the folks.

The throne of a heavy chair, cobbled together from scraps of lumber, sits off to my right about thirty feet away from the Lookout. It will be a dear friend during my stay, its broad armrests can simultaneously hold binoculars, a book, a journal, beer, and a pipe for smoking pot.

I savor a few moments of just standing there. There is an expectation I will leave this place as a different man somehow, and so too a felt need to honor this arrival and to orient physiologically and emotionally before unshuttering the lookout and moving in.

Beauty and awe spread out over the beloved and familiar rugged landscape surrounding me, which drops away immediately on all sides, but for the ridge on whose knolled-end the lookout sits. From here, the ridge eases down to a saddle, then slowly ascends to higher peaks that lay eastward, and from whose summits the land plunges off into the renowned Middle Fork of the Salmon River Drainage. My old Forest Service assignment at the South Fork Guard Station, summers of '68 and '69, is down the South Fork Canyon, several river miles to the north. Further yet down river, at Mackay Bar, the South Fork joins with the Main Salmon River, the River of No Return, as it came to be known due to the fierceness of its waters and the ruggedness of the country.

My imagination lays a landscape of history onto the topography under my feet. It provides a window into the deeper enchantments of the area, including the habitation of the country by early exploring Native Americans. Later it was home to the Nez Percé, for whom it is still a sacred homeland. Lewis and Clark's expedition in 1804/5 opened the territory to exploration and exploitation by European descendants, like my own pioneering family ancestors.

To my north is also the expansive landscape and topography of the Frank Church Wilderness Area. To my west, across the South Fork River, rises the dramatic granite-faced Lick Creek summit, on the other side of which the earth descends to my winter home of Long Valley and McCall. South and up-canyon lay the Krassel Ranger Station, the historic old mining towns of Yellow Pine and Stibnite, few roads, fewer people, and lots of remote country—my kind of country.

Once settled into my summer home, my days easily fill with routines of memorizing subtle details of the mountainous river-break country for more easily reporting potential fire locations, watching the weather and praying for dramatic lightning storms, annual maintenance chores like painting the lookout, reading Carl Jung, Joseph Campbell, Carlos Castaneda, Jack Kerouac, Robert Bly, Gary Snyder, and Edward Abbey, journaling, and writing about my journey of learning to heal the Jehovah Wound. And there is the daily mile-round hike to the nearby spring for drinking and washing water.

At night, I step out the lookout door and lay on the ground, or sit in my chair, and lose myself in beauty and awe. The stars are clear and brilliant: billions of red, blue, and white diamonds, embedded in a sea of black, blink, twinkle, and sing, as if in a cosmic symphony. I want to reach out with my hand and stir the cream of the Milky

Way—my home galaxy among what, one hundred billion of 'em? *How many is that?*

And is it up I reach, to touch them, or might it be down I reach? It doesn't matter. I stand within the Milky Way, on this mountain peak, and at the center of the universe. And though it is a peak humanly significant only for its magnificent view of miles upon miles of wild forest lands, here I feel Earth herself afloat in a vast cosmic sea of wonder and mystery.

I am here to soak this in. More deeply. And to learn from the magnitude of this mystery, to realize more fully what it is to be human. The identity story of my inheritance I am yet learning to release. I want a new story. A story that is real, true, and reflective of the magnificence I've touched—in the eyes and breath of Bear, within my breath on the cliff face, during the ecstasy of sex, or in those moments when separation between self and the unspeakable mystery, just disappear.

From my throne of scrap wood, I look out and see beauty everywhere. I am surrounded, immersed, and awash in a sea of mountains, pine trees, red, purple, and yellow wildflowers, and clean, crisp air with the smells of forest and mountain showers. The Sun's rays stream down like a cloudburst of light, warm on my skin. Sitting meditatively with legs crossed, I feel my face, arms, chest, and legs—my entire naked body—all caressed by sunlight. Recent readings in quantum physics inform and invite me to experience light's waves actually passing through the illusionary solidity of my body.

This somatic altered state effects of the mushrooms are familiar to me: the light queasiness in the pit of my stomach, the tightness in my chest—inviting consciousness of breath, the heightening of sensory acuities. The buzzing of insects takes on species-specific signatory vibrations my body recognizes. The air smells of forest, life, and promise. Colors brighten and strengthen the subtle varieties of sky blues and forest greens. Towering cumulous clouds tumble, a tumultuous swirling mass of boiling energy, made visible in a dance of whites and grays and blacks. The clouds cast shadow shapes onto the landscape below them. Shapes that flow over the mountains, over the steep-sided South Fork Canyon and its dendritic drainages. Rain falls out of a cloud on the other side of the river canyon. The bottom just drops out of the rolling-boiling thunderhead like a dark sheet falling from the sky. Blue-black expanses of water fall by gravity's grace, blown by the wind into sensuous shapes that billow outward as they fall earthward from their birth in a cloud so alive I can barely stand to look upon such beauty, such raw, humbling thundering power. Mountaintop vistas can be like this.

I ask the mushrooms to teach me about life, about the ways of the forest. I pray and plead for wisdom, so I can see and know the ways of Life, and her mysteries.

I see inside my body. This body, sitting cross-legged in a funny-looking throne of a chair, and I see mountains and rivers, forests, deserts and seas, storms and quiet, moons and tides, stars and galaxies—inside.

What is outside me, this world, this planet, this cosmos, is inside, too. It is a cosmos of fractals and holograms. This beauty that I stand in sheer awe of outside me, I too, am. My body is the world. I am its lover.

Why is it such a struggle, so hard, to love yourself, Larry? I ask this of my soul, like a mantra. Every day, like a child writing the question of his heart on a blackboard—again and once more, I ask this question of my soul: *Why is it so hard to love yourself?*

I drop back into childhood experiences. Into all the pains of betrayals and griefs and sorrows of my adulthood too. The memories are like a river that washes me to the sea, with anger and resistance back to being a kid. To being property. To having to be what I am not. To being so concerned with what people will think of me—the preacher's kid—I am forbidden to explore outside the boundaries of who I am supposed to be. Of what I might like or want. I fall back into being so afraid of God, of Dad, of the Devil, that their faces merge into one as I fear for my life during dangerous days and nights of terror. "If you die tonight, where will you spend eternity?"

Life itself feels like a trap, which is too frightening to face, so I turn it inside out and hate myself. It is me that is flawed.

My spirit and soul are exhausted from this battle against self-hatred. So I surrender like a drowning person giving themselves up to the ocean. This is what I came here for—to see if I could plumb these depths, to see if I might discover a way through my recurrent bouts of self-loathing. The waves lap over me. At first, I fight to keep my head up, but it is too much. I am tired. I have no energy, no will left with which to fight. I cannot keep the water out of my mouth or my throat. Coughing and sinking, I inhale my first lungful of water. Now I breathe water—*the only way through my pain and dogged self-despising must be into it, through it. I must embrace it*, I think.

If I am to know it fully, I must say "Yes!" to it. So I let myself hate myself.

Now, on the exposed ridgetop, I lay my naked body on bare Earth and cry. I grovel in the dirt and sob. Cry the tears I forbade myself as a child. Shame and guilt, anger and hatred, disdain and repugnance of people and society lay claim inside my body to unworthiness and never belonging.

"If you die tonight, where will you spend eternity? Don't let this opportunity to be right with God pass you by. He loves you. He wants you. Eternal life can be yours if you will but believe, confess your sins, and be baptized."

"Or, maybe you've left the fold, erred from the way, and just need to ask God for forgiveness. Come down the aisle tonight and we will pray for you. Don't let this chance for eternal life with God pass you by."

"Jesus died for your sins that you might have everlasting life with God in Heaven. Accept him now as your savior lest you spend eternity in fire and brimstone tortures of Hell."

The last air expires from my lungs, bubbles rise to the ocean's surface. I sink yet deeper, wonder that any light at all reaches these depths. *Help me understand*, I pray to the universe. *Teach me about life*, I plead.

They say that drowning is like falling asleep, that it becomes a peaceful experience. Perhaps that is why I fell into a quiet peace inside. I see that I live—from the inside out. I witness inherited beliefs, perceptions, and attitudes shape and color the stories of identity I live, my interpretations and expectations of people, life, and the world. I witness the choice to choose willingness—the willingness to suspend identity, to release the security of my hold on knowing.

Within the psychedelic moment, I encounter belief, experience, and language entwined in a co-creative process—the way a forest is more than a tree, chipmunk, sunshine, or rain. The way a squirrel secrets away a tree's nuts for its winter stash, some of those seeds becoming trees, feeding descendant squirrels in the sun, and rain.

I am no more an object than is Forest. I too am an ecological process of flows, creating inside the very mirrors through which I interpret the world outside! The ancient Hermetic phrase comes to mind, *"As above, so below. As within, so without...."*

And as I sit in the scrap wood throne, I experience this ecological nature of my being in a dynamic process. It is not merely a theoretical or intellectual thing. It is a somatic cellular experience of stumbling upon my consciousness in the act of creation—procreating the self-structure of Larry.

I feel like a little boy stumbling upon a leprechaun in the green forest; the elfin being looking up in surprise, caught in the act of ritual creation. The mushrooms do this for me; open this world of deep perception.

From my exposure to Aldous Huxley and his book, *The Doors of Perception* (Huxley 1954), Carlos Castaneda's works, and others, such as F. Bruce Lamb's, *Wizard of the Upper Amazon* (Lamb 1971), I know the eating of psychedelic mushrooms is an ancient and honored shamanic practice. Magic mushrooms, as they were commonly called, were a legendary party drug of the sixties and seventies. What we lacked, however, was mentorship in the ways of their venerable usage. Still, my novice experiences under their influence make risking their illegality seem to me an act of political defiance and spiritual assertion.

I imagine myself as a heroic and budding shaman. Consuming the dried earthy-tasting fungi requires a willingness to surrender to powers larger than the *I* of my construction. It is to invite in the willingness to enter unknown realms and dimensions, the willingness to transform, to see self and the world differently. Nothing in my Sunday church services, nothing in the ritual partaking of the body and blood of Christ, the bread and wine of the Eucharist, prepared me for the ecstasies and agonies of partaking of the holy mushrooms. (We used grape juice in church during our communion services since wine is a tool of the Devil. When Jesus turned the water into wine, it wasn't strong like the wine we make today.)

Years later, under their influence, I asked them to show me the true spirit, the true face of alcohol. In the solitude of wild desert darkness, with eyes closed, I repeat this prayer again and again, my body breathing into internal stillness, to better listen to what the mushrooms may show me.

A beautiful, seductive dancing, and half-naked woman appears before me. She spins and twirls, flirts with her eyes seductively looking into mine, clearly dancing for my attention and pleasure. Her eyes hold mine as her mouth comes in close for a kiss—and now a spin brings her face back up close to my own. In place of lips of love and pleasure are long bloody fangs and a hungry tongue, a fiery life-and-soul devouring monster, thrusting her all-consuming horrid face into mine. Such was the seductive *true face* of alcohol in my life in those days.

During my days on the lookout, I drink alcohol as medicine for my recurring bouts of loneliness and depression, as if its spirit might help me find my own. And I mix its liquid fire with my psychedelics, marijuana, and hash. I am a madman dreaming of claiming a life of my own. I want to steal it back, out from the grips of Dad's wrath and from the unjust and evil God of my youth. The one who foretells of his people in righteous battle against those who do not rejoice in his exaltation, "Their children also will be dashed to pieces before their eyes; Their houses will be plundered and their wives ravished" (Isaiah 13:16).

I hunger to see and know the true face of this God!

Tall cumulus thunderclouds build early this morning. Their beauty and promise of tumultuous, wild power entrances me. Through the day, they boil and billow to greater heights. Their earthward face grows ever darker, blacker. The anticipation of fierce lightning and thunder, and driving rains and winds, excites my hopes. *I love storms. This might be my night to do the big hit—if only the storm does not break until dark and it's too late to report any ignitions.*

I spend my day with this hope and watch fury grow with a promise of unleashing itself, journal some, work on the book I promised to write the night I ran away from home, and read. *I want to understand the Bible—the truth of who this God is, what the two conflicting Genesis stories of creation reveal. The two forbidden trees in the Garden—what are they about? And the serpent—who the hell is this serpent in the story? What's the energy he carries?*

"The Devil, Satan," I hear my father's voice answer. But I wonder. *What of the stories of the Serpent being a consort of the goddess? And why is Jehovah kicking Adam and Eve out of the Garden?*

"Behold, the man has become like one of Us, to know good and evil. And now, lest he put out his hand and take also of the tree of life, and eat, and live forever" (Genesis 3:22).

Who is this 'us' and why, or what, is God really afraid of here? Forbidden questions indeed!

Dusk falls and the clouds descend to within the reach of intimacy, and I decide to partake of the sacrament, to eat from the forbidden fruit of the *flesh of the gods* (Schultes, Hoffman 1979) (McKenna 1993). Their crumbly, fleshy dryness tastes of earth and soil. I wash them down with beer. Follow that with some hits of pot from my antler pipe.

And the world cracks open with an explosion of light and thunder. That thunder rolls into the distance, even as the next explosion is a bomb going off immediately overhead with simultaneously blinding light. The immediacy of the storm's presence enthralls me. There is no distance between us.

Wind and rain unleash themselves out of blackness in sheets of horizontally driven water. Bullets of rain explode upon impact against the ground and against the lookout's windows and roof. The force of the rain creates a deafening roar in concert with the continuous booming and rolling of thunder into the distance—and blasts of such frequent lightning that make for near daylight visibility.

And it all smells good, sweet, like rain and pine and freshly washed mountain air, rich with a new load of ozone. In this storm, I stand out of the wind and rain as best I can, just under the southern eave of the lookout. And I cheer and dance and scream with mad joy for more with each lightning strike. Being on initial attack for lightning-struck fires, over the years, placed me in the middle of many fierce storms—but this is the hottest storm of my life. And I am in ecstatic humility, filled with awe of such power and ferocity.

As if to match the storm's energy, I scream at God, fueled by the incredible fierce magnificence and wonder I am awash in.

"Go ahead! Kill me if you want," I yell. "I don't believe in you, anyway! If you are real, you can send me to hell, but you can't make me love you. You are a tyrant. You can't have my heart. You're nothing but an egotistical, over-inflated human ego. You're a human creation, aren't you?"

But as I howl into the fierce maelstrom at this God of my youth, this God lodged in my soul, I begin to feel his presence. I grow quiet and attentive inside. Looking. Listening. *There's something out there, yeah.*

Then I begin to see his image. Out there. His face in the clouds, his eyes. *Yes! There you are! In the clouds, just in front of me. Like you're suspended in hyperspace. And you're looking me straight in the eyes!*

The oft-heard phrase from childhood runs untethered and repeatedly through my mind. *"No man can look into the eyes of God and live."*

"I've conjured you up, haven't I! Called you in, huh? You here to kill me—cause I'm gonna tell the world what a fake you are? Afraid, are you?"

There is no shrinking back from the fear within me. Rather, I grow more confident of my suspicions and receive new confirming depths of insight into God's nature. "You're not only a creation of human needs, fears, and imaginations. But this same human energy that creates you, sustains you. Feeds you."

"Yeah! You're a parasite! A predator! I see you now! Feeding off the very human insecurities you create! You live inside me. Us. Tell us we're not enough. Call us sinners. Threaten us with eternal damnation if we don't bow down. You're an insecure fucking fraud!"

"But you're real too, huh? I see that now. You're an energetic force independent of us humans too—like a force in the universe. A real paradoxical illusion and delusion—all in one. You're a real historical constellation of collective unconscious powers to be reckoned with. Dangerous. Honored, somehow, but I will not bow down in praise and exhalation."

God! I marvel at my own human psychic, capable of creating in some deep unconscious shadowy realms that which it will then worship. Project the image outside of self—name it and then pretend one has not just created an internal concretized idol. And so also forget that naming and knowing—are not the same. It's easier to create gods than face the nakedness of not knowing!

It's like, like thought itself—creates experienced reality. The energy of a thought takes on vibrational independence apart from the thinker, and in this way has the power to hurt, or beautify, in the world. And with intent, it can be released like an arrow! God! How much more conscious I need to become of my own thinking, my thoughts...

"I see you, God! You're like the Roman two-faced god, Janus, aren't you? I see your mirror image. You're the devil, too! Aren't you? Yeah, you can't exist without an equal polarity, can you? Good and Evil are entwined, aren't they? We can't believe in one without creating the other, can we?"

"How convenient for you to have humans blame the world's evils on this other face, while you claim all the glory. You need each other—you are each other! And so, we human worshipers become just like you, huh? Hiding from ourselves and others what we don't want to look at, already living within. Damn!"

I keep staring into the eyes of the face in the nearby floating water vapors. They boil and roll through it—but the face stays in place. My spirit cries out to its spirit: "Let me see your true face. Who are you, really?"

This is a deep inquiry for me—the questions from the depths of desperation in my very being—listening comes from the same. "Who are you really? Let me see your true face. You're not even from Earth, are you?"

"No. You're from... some other place. You're like an alien, feeding on human fear and terror. You're neither of this world nor its creator, are you?"

"Who are you—and what's your grudge against women? Against the goddess? Why do you elevate the masculine over the feminine?"

"You command of followers to have no other gods before you. So—there are other gods! Why are you so jealous?"

The flashes of lightning and their explosions are simultaneous. And nearly continuous. There is no suspense of counting seconds after thunderous, forked lightning pierces the air before its physical impact hits my body. Thunder's booming hurts my ears. Darkness and light dance before my eyes and in my body.

"Yeah! Do it again! Yahoo!" I scream into the storm. I feel like I am riding a mountain top the way a bull rider precariously sits atop a dancing and twirling mass of angry flesh. No sooner does this heroic cowboy image flash into my mind than somehow, through my drugged consciousness, I became aware that the electricity in the air is... palpable.

I'm standing in it. Breathing it. Swimming in it!

My eyes look groundward. *I'm dancing up and down on the thick copper ground line for the lookout!*

It is not just God I am challenging, offering my mortal life to in exchange for an intimate conversation with, but the laws of the physical universe as well. Laws like gravity, that say if you are stupid enough to jump off a high cliff, you will lose. Laws that say lightning often strikes the highest thing around and it will flow off my little lookout structure right through this ground line under my feet.

Enough stupidity, Larry! RUN! RUN!

I dive in through the lookout's door, aiming for the rubber insulating mat, just as the bolt hits.

But my night is not over. I hoped to see ball lightning come into the lookout and bounce around, as in stories I'd heard, now that I was safely standing on my insulating mat. But I am not obliged. And such conversations with deities are exhausting. I am whipped. Beat up. I was about to try and put myself to bed, hoping to pass out, when I felt a presence behind me.

I turn to the door. Shiva walks in. Yeah. Right through the door comes the Hindu god of creation and destruction.

You might say I am hallucinating. Perhaps. Obviously. That is what I think too, at first.

He has all his arms out and about, just like in the pictures. One brandishes a sword. He lays that aside, sets it on the table by the wood stove, and attacks me. Jumps me. We fall to the floor and wrestle. I know I wrestle for my life. But I am no opponent for him. Still, he makes me struggle, as if playing with me.

Shiva puts me in a headlock. He holds me easily with only one of his many arms. From atop me, he applies painful pressure, tilts and turns my head until... until one further simple, subtle turn will snap my neck. And we both know it.

Now, he demands of me, "Do you want to live?"

I can barely breathe. It is all I can do to force out the words, "Yes! I want my life."

I struggle for another breath, struggle to get out what I know has to come next. "And—I am yours!"

"Yes, you are," he says. And I feel him smile as he releases the twisting of my head and neck.

Eventually, I fall into a fitful, dream-filled sleep.

You are fucking crazy, Larry. Insane, I say of myself on waking. Memories of the night before return like a flash flood in a rocky creek bed—me looking into the eyes of God, talking with him, challenging him like that, daring him to take my life, dancing on the grounding rod. Flashbacks and recollections, some vague, some clear, of what feels to be new knowledge, wash through me. I remember Shiva coming right through the door, the fight, the feel of my neck ready to snap, his asking—and my clear answer, *"Yes, I want my life."*

My body aches all over, and I am covered in bruises. I move slowly from the pain of it all.

Soon after my encounter with God, a phone call changes my life. The FS radio crackles. "This is Krassel. Come in, Glover. Yeah, Larry, we've got a request for you to call Rocky Kimball. We'll leave a truck with a phone in it at the trailhead. You can hike down and drive up to the summit to make the call."

I do.

"Hey Larry," Rocky says. "I'd like to hire you full-time come September. What'd think?"

Rocky, or Rok, or Dr. Richard Kimball, is the Director of the Santa Fe Mountain Center (now the Mountain Center). I've not held a year-round full-time job since leaving the Detroit Runaway House as Clinical Director eight years earlier.

The conversation pauses momentarily as I catch my breath, surprised by the offer. "I'd love to, Rok. Thanks!" And so, my seasonal stint the previous winter, as an Experiential or Wilderness Therapist, turns into a real profession and continuing to get paid to be in the wilds of nature.

I never thought I'd do therapy again, after leaving The Runaway House, what with my confusions and frustrations with the ambiguities of what helping really is. But introducing people to the world of nature—the very world that continues to save my life—and using adventure-based programming like backpacking, solo experiences, rock climbing, and running wild rivers, to be able to more formally study the dynamics of the human psyche, to work with juvenile delinquents, kids in lock-up, or men from the state forensic hospital, the "hospital for the criminally insane" for fifteen-day trips into the wilds of nature…

YES!

It was the winter of 1981 that life's synchronicities led me to meet Rocky and get hired to work a fifteen-day wilderness program with men from the New Mexico State Forensic Hospital. The men were placed there due to traumas suffered in the recent violent riots at the penitentiary in Santa Fe, where some thirty-three men died. On my first day on the job at the Center, I walk into the gear room to meet my partner for the upcoming fifteen-day program, which will be in Big Bend National Park, TX.

I meet Steve Waldrip there, where he is packing food, and filling zip locks with portions of granola, gorp, bagels, and such. Steve and I get to know each other as folks do.

It doesn't take us long to discover our shared family roots in Texas. Questions lead to answers that lead to further questions. "You went to Abilene Christian College? So you grew up in the Church of Christ?"

"Yeah," Steve says. "My dad was an Elder in the Church of Christ."

"My dad was a Church of Christ preacher! I was born in Abilene when he was in college there." My mind and heart swirl. I am thirty years old and have never met anyone else who left the church. Not in the roughly twelve years since I was ostracized. No one! I am in shock—and filled with joy and curiosity to explore Steve's story. What brought him to leave the church? To take on this journey into anathema, to be "cast out as one for whom it would be better to never have been born."

I'm not alone! Suddenly I feel a hope not known before. *Maybe I'm not crazy! I'm not the only one!*

A Great Amnesia

Once upon a time
Long and lingering ages ago

And not further away than today
A great historical and theological amnesia

Released itself upon the land of human creatures
That like a virus of the heart and mind

Yet stalks destruction of all worldviews but its own
Claims existence of none but this one true angry vengeful God of love

White and male he is too and
Gifts or perhaps curses those made in his image

Dominion over women and the rest of nature too
War is declared against the evil ones who bow not

And so a binary world of us against them is woven as
Followers succumb to infections of fear, submission, and domination

Still forgotten shadows bring holy invitations of suffering
for remembrance of magnificent sacred origins

An ancestry of innate divinity already living within
All that is

And so this dogma of the great forgetting
Sows the seeds of its own demise

For who can long thrive
Without honor for the cosmic womb of their birth

Their very selves already born into innate belonging and worthiness
Without Separation

From the heart that knows re-storying
Oneness with the sacred feminine is our path home

Chapter 2

CREATION STORIES—THE BIRTH OF A SELF

"Don't leave me!" I plead.

Mom wants to leave me with these people I don't know.

I don't know that I am a PK, a Preacher's Kid, yet either, being too young for such knowledge and still in training. This is one of my earliest life memories with any tangibility, and it is Dad's first Sunday as a preacher at this new church. It might have been one in the many hundreds of small West Texas towns.

The folks just converted from the Anti-Sunday School Church of Christ, where Dad had a job preaching, in Stillwater, OK. The *Anti's* don't let women teach Bible classes for their kids because the Bible forbids women to speak in church, you know. First Corinthians 14:34-35 says "Let your women keep silent in the churches, for they are not permitted to speak; but they are to be submissive as the law also says. And if they want to learn something, let them ask their husbands at home; for it is shameful for women to speak in church."

Anyway, as I later learn, Dad and Mom decided, after great Bible study and prayers, that it is not a sin for women to teach Bible stories to children in church—so long as no men are there. She's excited that Bible classes will now be part of her children's church life, but when she goes to leave me in that little room with all those strange kids and the stranger woman, well... I cry. I am three years old.

Mom half-drags me outside. We are on the concrete front steps of the little white church building. People stand around visiting as they arrive for the regular worship service. She whips off one of her high-heeled shoes for this spanking and uses the sharp tapered end. I dangle and squirm as I try to avoid the incoming blows, suspended mid-air between heaven and earth, by one arm. She hollers at me in front of everyone. "You're a bad boy, Larry. Bad boy. Now stop crying."

Everyone watches the new preacher's wife with the youngest of her three children. I feel their eyes. My body burns hot with the fire of shame, and my soul too, there on the steps of God's church. I want to run.

Fire and I, shame and I, we go all the way back to creation, together.

Two more moves to bigger towns and churches and we land in a railroad and ranching town in SE Colorado. Dad makes church memberships grow fast. He is always out studying the Bible with people, converting them to the Church. He is so good at this that we need to build a real church building and they even built a preacher's house next door too. Now, Benny, he's the oldest, and I each get a bedroom in the basement and there is a larger room for Bible classes there too. Kay, the next oldest, has her own room upstairs.

On Saturdays, we clean the church building auditorium and classrooms and straighten chairs. Church is our home.

I don't do well in school, however. And with our move into the new preacher's house, now that we live on the borderline between schools, Mom thinks I should get a fresh start at a new school. I like the building at my new school because it is old and made from big stone blocks and has a good playground including a tall slide you can burn your butt on. I also like the long walks to and from school—they give me time to be alone.

What does not work for me is school itself. I get into fights and just skip occasionally. I hang out at the park, or the Clay Hills, a great place without any houses where I look for fossils, arrowheads, horned toads, snakes, and things.

My teacher—she doesn't like me. I don't like her either. I don't know how to do math. I can't spell either. I don't understand the made-up rules. I don't like school.

But I have a new friend now. I even stopped by his house with another boy once and he invited us inside. "Want to see a hangman's knot?" my new friend asks.

I figure every cowboy needs to know this knot, so of course I say, "Yes!"

Mom calls me to come into the kitchen. Dad sits at the table, next to her. I am in trouble. They don't talk to me alone like this. Ever. Unless I'm about to get a whipping. I am scared.

"Sit down," Mom says. I sit in the chair across from them, swinging my legs above the floor.

"We're going to hold you back a grade." Mom continues. "You're not flunking," she offers for reassurance. "We just want you to get better grades."

"But you can go to a new school. We are on the borderline for all three schools, and this is a better school for you, Larry. It's called South School. And you can make new friends. No one will know you're taking the third grade again and…"

That's a lie. Everyone will know it, I tell myself. They release me from the prison of my chair. *They don't like me, Mom and Dad. I make them feel bad, I can tell. I had just made a friend at Park School too!*

I go to the alley where a neighbor piled the fall leaves off their yard between two trashcans.

I curl up into a ball in the pile of leaves. They make room for me, crinkling and cracking when I move, but at least they are friendly and smell good.

I cry. *Mom and Dad—they don't like me. I bet I'm not really their son. They don't love me, else they wouldn't hit me like they do.*

I didn't ask to be born. You didn't ask me, God. I hate you! You're not fair. You're not good!

I hate you, Mom, and you too, Dad. I didn't ask you to be my parents. I didn't ask to be born.

I don't want to be alive. I just want to die. I hate myself.

There's something wrong with me. I know there is. Nobody wants me.

Maybe... yeah, I could take the rope and the ladder in the garage and I can hang myself from one of the rafters there. Yeah. I can kill myself. I can tie that knot, I bet.

That will teach them. Then they'll be sorry they weren't nice to me.

Maybe there really is something special about me, though, and they just can't see it. Someday, though, someday if I grow up, I'll do something special, and I'll be a hero and then they'll see—then they'll wish they loved me now.

I hate you both. I hate being alive. I hate you too, God. I didn't ask to be born. You're not good.

I could take that rope... I imagine tying the hangman's noose, climb the ladder, and put the rope over a rafter in the garage and put my head into the knot. *I want to be dead.*

I cry myself to sleep, lying alone in the pile of leaves, there in the alley between the two trashcans out behind the preacher's house.

"We just moved here from Texas," I lie to the kids at the new school.

"Yeah, we had a ranch there. I have my own horse." *It's a sin to lie but... I am bad, but...* I just want to belong, be like the other kids, not the preacher's kid.

Dad says, "Texas is God's country," so I feel proud to say, "I'm from Texas." It makes me feel important. The Bible says pride is a sin, but Davy Crockett died at the Alamo in Texas, and he's my hero.

"Line up in single file, kids," the teacher orders into the pandemonium as we are joined by a second class. Then we are herded off to another building and into a large room. It has gray, square linoleum tiles on the floor, and it's cold in there. Stacks of gray metal folding chairs, like we use at church, lean up against one wall.

There are more kids here than I've ever been with in one place before, except on the playground, maybe. The kids are all excited and noisy and act like a bunch of anxious calves who don't know what's going to happen next. It's my first day at the new school.

"Okay, line up in two rows, beginning right here. Girls here, and boys here," one teacher yells to the babbling mob. We line up, and I am across from a pretty girl with eyes sparkling with blue light and a smile as big as Texas. Her blond hair is in a ponytail down to her waist. I like that. It moves every time she does.

"Hi," she says, looking me straight in the eyes. Her eyes go right through me. She doesn't blink or look away and her smile is fearless and inviting too.

She reaches out and offers me her hand at the teacher's instruction. She is not even scared. I stand... stupid. No one has ever looked at me like this before, straight in the eyes with an open invitation for play and joy dancing out of her very gaze.

Another teacher walks fast, like she is on a mission, into the large room waving a sheet of paper in her hands, calling out: "Larry Glover! Larry Glover. Where is Larry? Raise your hand." I think maybe God has found me out!

"I have a note from your parents excusing you from dancing. It is against his religion," she explains to everyone else in less than half a breath. Everyone stares at me just long enough to light my face and body on fire. I burn with shame.

I walk to the side of the room, unfold one of the cold metal chairs, and sit alone. The other kids laugh and have fun. I hide my eyes and stare at the gray floor, but no one looks at me, anyway. Not even the pretty girl with the dancing ponytail. I try to go invisible. *I want to die. I should have killed myself.*

They all know who I am now. I'm the preacher's kid. The PK. We don't believe in doing that stuff, in having fun that way. We're not like other people. We're different. We're God's people and it's not safe to let yourself play the way everyone else does. That kind of fun is dangerous.

I just wanted some friends. I would have given up all my special-ness just to belong! For a change. But dancing and playing like that is a sin.

I guess I was in the fifth or maybe it was the sixth grade, but on that day, I do not know how old I am. I only know I am innocent this time.

"Well then, this will get you for all the times I should have whipped you and didn't," Dad says.

Benny and I make a pact between us. "I'm not going to cry," Benny whispers to me, as though crying will betray the honor of our innocence.

"I'm not either," I say to Benny. I swear inside too. *I'm never gonna give him the pleasure of my pain or tears again.*

Benny goes first. He is the oldest, and it is part of the ritual. I sit waiting on the floor in the hall, my back next to the wall for support, next to the door outside Mom and Dad's bedroom. That's where we go for spankings like this.

We go to church that night like every Sunday night. Dad preaches. He is big and tall and is a giant in the pulpit, and everyone listens to him.

"We don't need no fancy electric dishwasher in my home. I've got five kids and they're all run by switches." He jokes. *He jokes! Laughs! And they are all laughing with him!*

He looks at me, in the audience, and I feel everyone else look at me too. My face is so hot with fire that I think I might burst into flames right there in the church pew. Some kid at school said that happens to people sometimes. *Spontaneous combustion*, he called it.

But right now, my shorts stick to my skin, and sitting on the hard wood pew hurts, and I want to change positions—but I dare not move. Everyone will see any move at all I make. I feel their eyes burning into me already.

Dad now holds his black leather Bible up in the air for all to see the authority he speaks and quotes from. Dad speaks for God.

"First Corinthians 11, verse 3: 'But I want you to know, that the head of every man is Christ; and the head of woman *is* man; and the head of Christ *is* God.'"

"This is God's model: Man is the head of the household even as God is the head of Christ. And God declares: 'Children, obey your parents in the Lord, for this is right.' Ephesians 6, verse 1."

"And in Proverbs 23, verses 13 and 14, God says, 'Do not withhold correction from a child, for *if* you beat him with the rod, he will not die. You shall beat him with the rod, and deliver his soul from hell.'"

"God has prepared the place of Hell for those who do not obey him, a place of everlasting torture and torment, a place of fire and brimstone waiting for the ungodly."

I wait for Dad to point his finger at me from the pulpit, naming me among the ungodly, worthy only of Hell. Maybe then I can stand up and just confess. *I am a sinner. I'm not enough. I never will be. Never can be. I am less than a gnat in the eyes of God and I don't deserve his grace.*

"Parents are to discipline their children even as God disciplines us. It is out of love. God is love," Dad preaches on. "He sent his only begotten son so that 'He who believes and is baptized will be saved; but he who does not believe will be condemned.' Mark 16:16."

"Notice that '*and is baptized.*' God wants us all to be saved. That is why he gave us his holy word, word for word inspired by his very breath. Truth, so that we might have a path to freedom and salvation. If you follow it, 'The Truth shall make you free,' John 8:32."

But I do not feel free when Benny and I get ready for bed that night. *I am trapped in my shorts!*

"This is not right," I tell Benny.

Sixty-plus years later, Benny still remembers me telling him that.

But that night I tease my white shorts away from the oozing scabbing on my skin and it hurts. They stick to my skin with a red-tinged gooey fluid. *I hate God. I hate Dad. I hate myself. I hate life. I am... hate.*

One day, during the summer before we started the seventh grade, my friend Johnny called to tell me where and when I should meet him. Johnny and I were always having fun and getting into trouble together. With pride, he said he knew this girl who would "show us her tits." Fear and trembling and excitement moved me. With my feet peddling to go faster downhill, I rode my faded red Schwinn bicycle back over the bridge and across my friend, the Arkansas River. Johnny, I, and Diane all arrived at the barn together. I had never felt more awkwardly excited. But in the hayloft of a deserted barn, she took off her pink blouse first, and then her white bra.

"You want to touch them?" she asks. They are so big and beautiful. I don't know what to do with them.

I am an unprepared neophyte thrust into the presence of the Holy Spirit. Just looking at those holy breasts boils my blood and turns my brain into a hormonal stew. Afterwards, for days, my brain is single-focused. There is only me and those large naked breasts. In the whole of the universe. And the soft feel of her silky skin under my fingers. Her pink nipples.

God let the Devil put some powerfully tempting wicked pleasures in my body. Or else—God put them there Himself. What kind of God would do that?

Johnny's father and mine also have a relationship. Johnny's father liked his alcohol, and his mother was a member of the Church. My dad was forever trying to get Johnny's dad to give up alcohol and join the Church. Years later, Dad still loved to tell the story from the pulpit of driving Johnny's dad to the Veteran's hospital so Mr. Jones could dry out. Seems that on the way there, Mr. Jones left scratches on the dashboard of our station wagon from his fingernails desperately clawing while he begged my father to stop the car so he could get one last drink. He apparently did not know my dad like I did.

I cannot hear the story without finding myself back in the barn with Johnny, feeling some odd mixture of shame and pleasure. *Thinking evil thoughts is the same as doing them, is what the Bible says.* I remember.

If there had been a sex education class at school, us preacher's kids would have been exempt. On religious grounds. Like for dancing. And mixed swimming. Or for reading some books. *The folks are afraid the world out there will get into me somehow. It's evil out there. The world is not to be trusted.*

We move again. I am fourteen years old. I have lived in six places and the eighth grade here will be my sixth school. This time, we again move to a bigger church but also to, what is for me, a big city, a suburb of Detroit, MI. Dad says if he's going to convert more people to God, he needs to be where there are lots of people.

"Your Dad is a fisherman of men," Mom says proudly, referencing Mathew 4:19 and Christ's promise to his disciples to make them 'fishers of men.'

I write my name on the hood of the car in the black soot that comes from the car factory at the end of our block. The air is dirty here. I miss the big open plains of southeastern Colorado, the open lands I got to walk through. We lived in little towns before this. I want to be a cowboy and rodeo bull rider and know nothing about Pontiac GTOs and Firebirds. I don't know cars like the other kids do.

The church holds a Sunday picnic after services so the congregation can all meet the new preacher and his family. I hate these big gatherings, but the fried chicken and food are plentiful and good!

So, when I get out of the car—and there's a big green grassy park with lots of big trees and a tall slide and giant swings and climbing bars and church kids laughing and playing on 'em—I head over to join in.

One kid, near my age, is swinging higher and higher, and I think maybe he'll jump out but no. He's going higher yet and I can see he's going for a giant swing—going all the way over the top and back. He's getting close, and I've never seen anyone do it before and he comes flying in a high arc, right out of the swing and lands on the ground. Flat. With a thud.

I am closest by and run over quickly. The first thing I see is his right arm bent all out of shape, with two sharp bends in it. He is screaming in pain and holding his arm with his other hand and people are gathering round. His father is there now and commands, "Don't be a crybaby! Stop it right now."

The kid swallows hard and tries to hold back his sobbing even as rage rises in me like a volcano. God may not like crybabies, but I think I might scream, or maybe throw up. Instead, I just run away from the boy's pain and mean dad.

But I remember once walking with Dad on the sidewalk as a young one when we first moved to Colorado. I trip on a crack, fall hard, scared, and hurt myself. And I remember Dad bending down and commanding, "Stop your crying, now! Don't be a crybaby."

"Here, look here." He begins looking at the crack where I tripped, touching and rubbing it with his hand. Then he laughs and says, "Nope, you didn't hurt it at all."

He stops laughing and says, "Now stop your crying or I'll give you something to cry about."

Dad grows the membership at the new church rapidly, so they bought a preacher's house for us to move into, allowing the old preacher's house next to the church building to be used for classrooms. Soon after moving into the new house, however, Mom is driving us kids home after Sunday evening church services and there is smoke billowing out a window. Fire!

We move back into the old house and organize our lives around setting up and taking down chairs for Bible classes once again. It is a relief when we finally move back into the remodeled preacher's house.

Soon after, in confusion and fear, I wake one night in the underground blackness of my damp basement bedroom.

It is the restrained muffled voices in the kitchen above that wake me. The door at the top of the basement stairs is closed, so I strain my ears with attention to make out what is happening. The voices get louder.

That's Mom. She's crying. Sobbing!

And that's Dad—pleading, saying "Please!" Sounds like he's begging her. Please? What's going on? He sounds scared. And Mom, she's really hurting. I've never heard her cry like that!

"Just give it to me," I hear Dad say. "Just give it to me?"

Just give it to me? What's he talking about? There is a herd of thundering horses in my chest, the chest that holds its breath— listening.

"Stay away from me," Mom says. "Stay away from me." The words come out strong and fast and strung together, as if Dad is moving toward her.

Stay away from me? I know that's what she said. Stay away from me? What's going on up there?

My heart beats so loud it blocks my hearing. *What is she saying? Something about elder's wives and gossip?*

"Please, just give it to me." There's Dad again.

"I just want to kill myself!"

Mom! I screamed inside, but there was no breath inside for its escape.

She has a knife! That must be it! The butcher's knife! She's threatening to kill herself with the butcher's knife!

"I just want to kill myself," she sobs again. But in her saying it, and the creaking of the floor above, I know she is now crying into Dad's chest.

Their voices get quieter. More unintelligible. Mom is crying. I've never heard her cry before.

I remember the night was so black I could not see my hand at the end of my arm. I hold it out and look for it during the long night when I cannot sleep.

Everything is normal the next morning, except for something inside of me.

Later, I learn that some of the church women didn't like Mom's choice of color for paint in the kitchen and didn't mind publicly saying so. It was their house, after all, and we were just using it, apparently. Being a preacher's family was hard on all of us.

Oh, This Heart...

Oh, this heart of mine
this heart
shared by you too
she can be such a lonely hunter
looking for love, as they say
in all the wrong places
as though something inside
cannot see the source of its own hunger
being lived out in the roughs of a wild world
a world incapable of giving to a self
that will not first open
and ever so vulnerably and tenderly
courageously receive
from its own Being
that wholeness
that love
it most desires

Chapter 3

A WRETCH LIKE ME

Dad is on his way out of the house, his house, with his worn, black leather-bound Bible in hand. I am fourteen, maybe fifteen years old. He is leaving for a Bible study meeting with some people. He has Bible Study meetings every night and day of the week. He is converting so many people to the church that we even have two worship services on Sunday mornings now because we are outgrowing the church building. Mom is proud of him. I ask him if he will give me a ride someplace.

"No. I don't have time. I'm running late."

"You never have time for me," I risk.

"Listen, you are living in my house and eating my food. If you don't like it, you can leave. So long as you live in my house, you will do what I say when I say. Now stop your complaining. I have work to do. And I'm late."

I am so tired of you telling me this. I got things to do now too. I'm leaving! I hate you, I say to myself as we both turn toward the front door of the preacher's house. We are now a comedy act, Dad and I.

We reach the door together and try to squeeze through at the same time, bounce off the door jams and try again, bounce off once more in our race to leave, and then somehow slide out the door.

Dad gets in his car and drives off. I walk down the sidewalk in the opposite direction, cursing him and hoping he will look in the rearview mirror for his last-ever look at me. Then he can be sorry.

Goddamn you. I hate you. I didn't ask to be born. You had no right to bring me into this world and not love me. You don't love me. I'm never eating another bite of your God-damned food if it's the last thing I do. I swear at Dad.

I hate myself too. There is something wrong with me, I think, as I replay Mom telling us kids for the first time about Grandpa Glover, Jack Cole Glover. He killed himself with a gun.

I hear her again say, "He had a reputation as a hard man, even with animals. He was a horse trader, buying and selling horses, and breaking them first, sometimes. He liked to drink and gamble, and was handsome and something of a ladies' man."

Dad is driving, and we are on our way back to Texas to visit family for Christmas and Mom is explaining why we don't have a Grandpa Glover to visit. Dad doesn't say anything but keeps looking straight ahead, both hands on the steering wheel. Mom keeps talking.

"Anyway, he made a big sale and went out drinking and gambling afterwards with some bad women. Prostitutes." She stumbles over the word. "Women who sell themselves to men," she explains, in a way that does not invite questions. "They got him drunk. He lost everything in a poker game. They knew he had a lot of money on him and must have ganged up on him somehow. He must have got so desperate trying to get his money back that he bet the family farm. And they got that from him too. He went home and got a rifle and shot himself. Your dad was a freshman in college."

I see Grandpa in my mind's eye sitting in a smoky saloon scene from a *Gunsmoke* TV Western series, playing cards at the round wooden table, with whisky bottles and women with low-cut blouses there too. "I have his name, huh, Mom?" I say, feeling an immediate affinity for him.

"Well, yes, and you have his eyes. But you're named after my oldest brother, Jack, too," Mom mentions her brother Jack as if to distract me from bonding with a dead man, and a sinner at that. But she is too late.

I walk on and think, *I'm like Grandpa. We both like horses and girls, and I feel like an outlaw, and I might kill myself too, and … there is something wrong with the Glovers, something wrong with our genes. Dad never laughs. Grandma Glover is mean, and she never laughs either. There is something wrong with the Glovers. I hate myself.*

There is something wrong with you too, God. You are evil. I don't care what you say. I didn't ask to be born and now you threaten me with hell if I don't do what you say. Well, fuck you, God! I hate you too.

And so my mind races through the night as I walk the suburban streets into the evening hours. They are busy with people leaving and going to the factories. I cross the street in the middle of the block when I feel like it, right in front of the oncoming cars. I don't care if they hit me, but they stop suddenly, honk at me, and curse.

I give them the finger.

Then I see people eating dinner through the windows of their houses. The curtains close. *Maybe I can see a girl naked through the curtains! Maybe I really am like Grandpa Glover. I think about naked girls all the time.*

I'm such a sinner. Sex is all I think about. I walk around school with a hard-on. Rub my dick in pep rallies at school—watching those cute cheerleaders with their short skirts, showing off their naked legs and white panties, and dancing that way. Coming in my jeans and having to carry my books in front of my crotch to cover the wet spot. Shamed. Ashamed. Of my body. Of my desires. I'm such a sinner.

I didn't ask for a dick, God! And now you're going to send me to hell for having one! Fuck you, too. You and Dad are just the same: BASTARDS!

I hate life! I hate being alive. I hate myself! I'm just a worthless fucked up sinner. I should just kill myself. There is something wrong with me, isn't there God?

I'm hungry and lonely and want to die. Lights in the houses are going off and the streets get darker and silent. Traffic ceases. I imagined people curled up in their beds, stomachs full.

Wonder where I can go? How will I eat? Where can I sleep? Nobody will give me a job. I'm too young, and he knows it. He knows that! "As long as you live in my home..." If I get picked up by the cops, they'll just take me home, and then Dad will beat me and maybe lose his job because of me—and then where would we live? And all because of me.

The night grows long. I grow tired. Exhausted. I have nowhere to go. No one to go to.

Are you real? I ask of God. *Like really real? Not like Santa Claus? Not make-believe? And all that stuff in the Bible—all that really happened just like it says, word for word?*

You made the world in six days and Adam and Eve, and they ate the forbidden fruit and Cain killed Abel and you repented that you had made man and Jesus died for my sins? For my sins. My sins. I don't want to go to hell, God. Bible verses play and replay through my head like songs stuck in repeat mode.

For the LORD your God is a consuming fire, a jealous God. (Deuteronomy 4:24)

O fear the LORD, you his saints! There is no want to those who fear him. (Psalms 34:9)

For all have sinned and fall short of the glory of God. (Romans 3:23)

For God so loved the world, that He gave His only begotten Son, that whoever believes in Him should not perish, but have everlasting life. (John 3:16)

Then Peter said unto them, "Repent and let every one of you be baptized in the name of Jesus Christ for the remission of sins; and you shall receive the gift of the Holy Spirit." (Acts 2:38)

Did you really send your son so I can be saved? Watch him suffer and die on the cross?

I see Christ, nails pin his hands and feet to the cross, blood drips from the spear wound in his side. *He is in pain, tortured for my sins. Suffering for my sins. So I can be saved. I need saving. I am evil. Worthless.*

"We are less than nothing to God, less than gnats, except for his grace. He is so great. God is love. Praise be to God." I hear a life full of sermons preached and Bible verses quoted. Over and over, they play in my head, along with gospel songs. *"Amazing Grace, how sweet the sound that saved a wretch like me. I once was lost…."*

I pray. *I want to be saved, God. I don't want to go to Hell. I'll give you my life. I'll even be a great preacher or missionary for you, like the prophets in the Old Testament. I'll have courage and be faithful, like Daniel in the lion's den or like David killing Goliath. I'll be a Fisher of Men for you. I'll be a great preacher or even a missionary. I can be even better than Dad. You can have my life; it's not any good now, anyway. I don't want it.*

I won't be like Jonah, scared to preach your word. You won't have to send me into any whale's belly. No, I'll be a great evangelist for you. You won't have to ask me twice.

There's just one thing, God. One thing I don't want to do. I don't want to have children, God. I think that would be a sin to bring them into the world—with the chance of them maybe going to Hell and all. It's too big a risk. This world is not, well, you know, it's not safe for human souls. Not with the Devil around trying to get us into Hell.

Well, I hope you understand about my not having any kids, God. But I'll do anything else you ask of me. I'll go to prison, and I'll even die for you. I'd like that. I can be great for you!

Maybe... maybe... maybe I really am special and just haven't learned it yet.

Maybe... maybe... maybe I'm really—you're crazy, Larry, no—maybe I am Christ come back, and I'm just now learning and remembering who I am. Yeah. Maybe I really am that special!

As if it were a nipple suckled on from birth for comfort and orientation of how to be in the world, my body replays this gospel song again and again: *Onward Christian Soldiers, marching as to war, with the cross of Jesus, going on before....*

Purpose and meaning return to my life with submission and repentance. So it is I re-enter the known world of my father's house as dawn arrives. Lights begin to come on in neighboring homes. The traffic is picking up for the early shift at General Motors. I open the back door as quietly as possible, sneak down the stairs to my bed, and wait for the soon-to-come voice of Dad at the top of the stairs. He will burst into song, singing the opening lines of *Oh, What a Beautiful Mornin'*, and follow them with, "It's time to get up, don't make me tell you twice!"

That morning, no one seemed to have even noticed my absence through the night. It was not like the return of the Prodigal Son; no fatted calf is killed in my honor and no feasting is to be had. Everything is the same in the house that morning, except me.

I am born anew.

I have a new identity, a new self. *I am a soldier for God in the war against the Devil, against evil. I've been chosen too, called by my God even, to be a great preacher, maybe even a martyr. Me and God. Me and Jesus. We're tight. We talk to each other. I might even be—well, I know it's crazy; I know it's a sin to think this, but maybe—I might even be Christ himself coming back. Could be I'm still just discovering who I really am—that I really am the Son of God! That's who I might be. Then people will love me...*

There is only one thing that stands yet between me and a new life, I figure. I think it best I get baptized again for the remission of my sins next Sunday—just to be sure.

I don't want a technicality to stand between me and salvation. I now figure that my first baptism, when I was in perhaps the fifth or sixth grade—well, I figure I was too young and didn't really know what I was doing. I didn't know there *really* is a spiritual war going on. But now!

I walk down the aisle during the invitational song the next Sunday morning, and Dad baptizes me by the scripturally required method of immersion in the baptismal tank behind the pulpit.

The original Greek word, translated as *baptism* in the New Testament, really means *immersion,* as Dad often explains from the pulpit. And so, we do it the way God intended, by immersion. No Catholic-like baptismal sprinkling for us!

Neither Mom nor Dad says anything to me about my new salvation—which disappoints me, and I find it a bit strange that they aren't happy for me and celebrating. I did just get saved from Hell. Right? *Maybe Mom will fry up a second chicken for dinner for the seven of us*, but no.

Still, the act signifies for me the birth of a new self, one with new loyalties. My declared loyalty is now officially to God, above any loyalty to men, or even to family or self. And thus, my loyalty is also to Truth and its freedom—and to their spread around the world. "… the truth shall make you free," John 8:32, as I learn to quote.

I get right to work studying the Bible, memorizing the required scriptures I need for converting people and for preaching. Within a couple of years, I have much of the New Testament memorized. I even buy myself a small, black, leather-bound New Testament, and a couple of Bible reference books, and now I dream of how God might use me.

I get to stand up front in church and help with the communion service, and lead songs and prayers too. I try to say beautiful and sincere prayers. God likes sincerity and I notice people compliment me for that too. I like that. It makes me feel important and powerful.

My commitment to this leadership role is synchronistic with a rising level of organized church youth activities in the tri-state area. This is the mid-60s and *TIME* magazine's cover boldly asks, *Is God Dead? (1966)* The article proceeds to write of "Christian atheism," a phrase that spins my head and provides plenty of preaching material for Dad.

The counterculture hippie movement is on the rise, along with the popularity of the Beatles and short mini-skirts, and Satan's liberal use of drugs as a temptation, exacerbated by disenchanted military veterans returning from a failed yet continuing and controversial undeclared war in Vietnam. President John F. Kennedy's assignation (1963) is followed by calls for and the assassination of Malcolm X (1965), the race riots in Detroit and elsewhere (1967), the killing of Martin Luther King, and then of Robert Kennedy in 1968.

It is a socially tumultuous time and the religious atmosphere within the church is one of anticipating the end times, one of soldiers of the cross preparing for spiritual warfare, of good against evil and us against them evil communists. There is also a new commitment to place more attention on youth activities.

Church-sponsored youth gatherings are held on weekend nights, with no drinking, drugs, dancing, or petting—to insulate us Christian kids from the viral influences of the world. Satan is loose upon the land and lurking about for souls to tempt onto the road of ruin and eternal torment.

It is within this environment that I ask our youth minister, now a dear friend of mine and typical of the really good-hearted folks in the church, to do me a favor when I have the honor of preaching one Sunday evening. I ask him to interrupt my preaching by walking down the center aisle from the back of the auditorium, at a designated point during the sermon. I write a note on a piece of paper and ask him to carry it in his hand where people will see it.

Now, our worship services are orderly and predictable in nature; no wild holy rolling or speaking in tongues or such for us. We know the flesh and emotions are not to be trusted; they can lead you astray and so disorder and chaos are of the Devil. So, Bill's behavior in the middle of my sermon brings the congregation of the faithful to an attention-filled silence. I stop preaching as Bill begins walking. Of course, I act innocent of any conspiracy and step out from the pulpit to accept the note he hands me. Adrenalin rushes through my veins as I play out the drama, try to breathe intentionally so as to control the shaking in my voice, slowly unfolding the paper, and read aloud.

"The note from Bill says: God has declared war against Satan. Against evil…"

Well, there are a dozen folks or so who come forward during the invitational song to recommit their lives to God after that sermon. My reputation as a fiery young preacher grows.

I like having people look up to me that way, respecting my commitment to God. Looking up to me when I stand in the pulpit—while I speak God's word to them. And I am making real friends too, church friends, but they are the first real friends I've had since moving to Michigan from Colorado. I belong now. Thank you, God.

I get more invitations to preach at other churches and at youth rallies. Once, I even spoke to several hundred kids—that scares me, but God is on my side, or rather, I am on his. "Not my will, but thy will be done, Oh Lord. Use me for your purpose…" to paraphrase Luke 22:42. I humble myself this way before God in my prayers, and then secretly hope the Almighty will use me in such a way that I will feel his power coursing through me and then people will look up to me even more.

God's power, working through me, converts twelve kids to the church in a year's time. This adds to my reputation too. One day I go to school only to learn that a fellow classmate has shot and killed himself the night before. Not unlike me, he was quiet and a skinny, bookish loner kind of guy, but I always made a point of saying "Hi" and being friendly with him, so I probably knew him as well as any of us.

That day, in English class, I sit down behind another lonely boy; Sam is skinny like me and usually walks the halls between classes alone, like me. He wears thick glasses and is one of us socially inept kind of guys. I figure him vulnerable to Christ's message of belonging. I imagine I can sense his loneliness and fears and his sins—and his readiness to accept Jesus as his savior.

"Hey Sam, did you hear about John?" I begin.

"Yea. Too bad, huh?"

"Did you hear how he did it?"

"Shot himself, I think."

"You ever hear about this really old book that tells you how you can live forever?"

"No."

"Yeah, it's like super old and ancient and is full of this secret knowledge. I got one. You want to meet me after school, and I'll show it to you?"

"Yeah. Sure."

I know then and there I'll be chalking Sam up on my board of converts that night, and sure enough, Dad baptizes him only a few hours later. I am proud. And then I try to hide my pride from myself, cause pride is a sin and even Dad never shows any pride in me for my preaching or converting.

Two church friends and I spend a summer month in a Northern Michigan tourist town to help a small church there prepare for a weeklong Revival Meeting. We go door-to-door to pass out Bible tracts and talk and study the holy scriptures with folks. I even travel to New York with Dad and other church folks to help spread the word for a weeklong Revival Meeting he is holding there. That is where I stand in front of a door when a kindly-looking older man opens it. I jump right in with my routine but immediately notice he never takes the gaze of his blue-gray eyes away from looking directly into mine.

"Hi. I'm here to let you know about a Bible Revival Meeting that is going on and I'd love to leave you with some information if you're interested. Or I could come in and study the Bible with you if you'd like?"

"No thanks," he says, with simplicity and no animosity and a simple disinterest. "I'm an agnostic."

"Uh, okay, thanks anyway. Have a nice day," I say and look up the word *agnostic* as soon as I have a chance. I didn't know but what it might be some kind of disease or something. But no; he wasn't sick, and neither an atheist nor a believer. I was prepared in my training and studies for people who say they don't believe in God, but nothing prepared me for someone who was willing to suspend belief and answers in the face of such stupendous monumental soul-defying questions of eternal magnitude.

Doesn't he know to answer true/false, yes/no, and good/evil, on the test question? You can either choose black/white, either/or. I never imagined one could slide through life answering, "I don't know," and live.

This simple encounter begins to provoke and awaken within me all the questions I began harboring since I was old enough to go to Bible School and wanted to ask, but was afraid to.

"Did the sons and daughters of Adam and Eve—you know—have to marry each other? Wasn't that a sin? How come their babies weren't—you know—like deformed and stupid or something?"

Or "So there weren't any rainbows in the sky until after the Flood and God repented and promised to never destroy the earth again that way?"

"Yes, Larry, that's right."

"Aren't rainbows made by the sun shining through the moisture in the air? So did it never rain before the flood?"

Questions! Damn questions. The more I study, the more they propagate! Worse than rabbits or Catholics!

"So, Dad, if the Bible is inspired word-for-word from God and we are to interpret it literally, well, how come the Bible says the 'sun stood still' when the Israelites marched around the city of Jericho?"

"Well, you have to use common sense, and anyone can see this is just a figure of speech."

"How about the six days of creation? Did God really make the whole universe in only 144 hours? What about those millions-of-years-old dinosaur bones in the museum back in Canyon, TX?"

Damn Questions! Asking questions can make you go to Hell if you aren't careful. Curiosity killed the cat, they say, and it got Eve into a whopping lot of trouble too.

I pray all the harder. "God grant me faith. I want to believe. I need to believe." I study harder too.

I grow bolder too, as if to compensate for my growing doubts, in my passing out of Bible tracts and trying to convert people to the Lord. I feel my heart race and face flush as I first make sure no one is around to witness, then leave *How to Be Saved* flyers in the bathroom at school.

And I make special trips to the drugstore to glance at photos of naked women—no, I mean in order to leave *How to be Saved* flyers in the centerfold page of Playboy magazines.

God, my face burns, and my dick makes an embarrassing bulge in my jeans. I try to walk out of the store all innocent, like nothing in *TIME* magazine interests me enough to buy it today. Then I go home and beat off and feel like such a wretch, such a worthless sinner. "God, please forgive me. I'll never do it again."

But I do.

We have a theology of fire. I don't want people to go to Hell. So, I do the work of God. Give people the Truth. I don't want kids to think I am a Jesus freak, though. We differ from them, and all the other so-called Christians too. We have the Truth. The *real* Truth. Not that hippy free-love truth stuff.

We're the Church of Christ and we are the True Church, the one-and-only True Church. Not the Baptists. Certainly not the Methodists or Lutherans, and especially not the pagan Catholics. They are spawned from the Devil, believing the Pope is infallible and that he speaks for God.

We are part of the historical lineage that broke away from the Catholics with Martin Luther, and then back to the nondenominational tenets of the first-century Christians through the likes of Barton W. Stone and Alexander Campbell in The Restoration Movement (1790-1840). Of course, we trace our true lineage back to the first Christians, the apostles and disciples of Christ's time.

We have the Bible, and we are the only ones who interpret and follow it word for word. We don't have instrumental music in our church services because the Bible doesn't say, "Lift up your instruments to God." It says, "Lift up your voice like a trumpet!" (Isaiah 58:1)

Our Sunday sermons are studies in such theological distinctions.

We don't play cards either. Or go to dances. The Devil just uses fun stuff like that to trick you into going to Hell.

God and the Devil are in a war. And they both want our souls. God made the Devil like he made us, I guess, but then…. Well, it gets complicated, but the Devil got jealous of man and wouldn't bow down to us, so God sent him to Hell. I guess God had to make Hell too, in order to send the Devil there, but then… It gets more complicated and such thinking is dangerous.

Just being alive is dangerous like that. You can do things you believe are right, but that will really make you go to Hell and you won't even know it until too late, like those Southern Baptists and Methodists and such.

You got to read the Bible right. Then you can see the Truth in it because God had 'em write it down word-for-word, straight from his lips.

I watch the lips of a beautiful girl. She comes unbidden to me at night, several times a week sometimes. She starts taking off her clothes and is getting right friendly with me, rubbing on me, and my body is building toward a release and—

God's voice explodes inside my skull, from out of nowhere. "If you do...," he warns while his giant finger thrusts itself into my face from out of the heavens. I wake sweating, and sit bolt upright in bed. Cold. Wet. The sheets are soaking wet. My hard penis aches for the explosion of pleasure.

I masturbate twice a day, first thing in the morning and last thing at night. More, when I find time to be alone. I pray for forgiveness. I am ashamed of myself. I have a dirty mind and a sinful body.

A Theology of Fire

I take a wooden match,
you know the ones,
with a red-head-capped-white.
Strike it on my jeans,
the way I learned,
with a boy's pride of achievement.

Anticipation watches flame
climb toward finger flesh,
feel the dancing fire and heat,
then drop it when
pain is too much.

I strike another.
hold it firmer
determined
until the flame dies
smothered by flesh!

I grow enamored of fire...
Hell fire and brimstone...
for an eternity...
"How long is that?"

"Another damn question!"
"And the innocent people, God?
Those that never even hear of you?
What about all those sincere people
who believe in you but don't...
you know...
get the Truth just right?"

Damn Questions!

Chapter 4

DAMN QUESTIONS

Between convulsions of doubt and belief, I aspire to be a famous preacher, missionary, or martyr for Jesus in the war against Evil. I take a speech class in the first semester of my senior year in High School. I sign up for it during a fit of passionate conviction. Must have figured the skills helpful—if my faith can just weather the storm. But when the teacher encourages me to enter a speech contest, I resist. I do not see how I can speak about anything other than Christ. I'm not sure I have the courage to do that.

What faith I have is held in place through sheer efforts of willpower. My soul is terrified. The foundations of my life are tenuous, as though the earth under my feet quivers in its orbit about the sun, perhaps even about to be flung into the cold, dark, deadly vacuum of deep space—at any moment! I do not know day to day, especially when the day for my speech comes, if I will be a believer or infidel.

The foundational beliefs of Christianity, as I know it, rest upon Christ's historical existence, and miraculous explanations of a virgin birth and his resurrection. I study and ponder the interrelated issues and questions. It is the same curiosity with which I approach anything that is broken, that I can get my hands on: a busted clock or radio with a broken tuning dial, or a malfunctioning lamp switch.

I love to take things apart, to see how they work. I pride myself on being able to figure out and fix most of what I dismantle. Mom jokes that, "You can break anything, Larry!" I figure if I can't fix it, I can at least have fun satisfying curiosities for how things work.

It is this curiosity, this hunger for understanding that leads me to consume C.S. Lewis's books, including *The Screwtape Letters* and *The Chronicles of Narnia*, in which, through fiction and allegory, he explores and affirms essential Christian theology. But then another book jumps off the library's bookshelf into my hands. It is Bertrand Russell's, *Why I'm Not a Christian*. I am intrigued by his purely rationalistic critiques of religion and of Christianity.

His disdain for organized religion, as being fear-based or emotionally driven, is new to me. And I am moved by the audacity of someone willing to stand before God and openly say, "I don't believe in you."

I've just never considered that someone could honestly study such issues, and based upon a reasoned intellectual assessment, choose not to be a Believer. I find myself questioning. *Who am I to question Russell's honesty and integrity?* The idea that there might be legitimate reasons for holding beliefs contrary to the Truth of my inheritance takes the intellectual and religious confidence out of me the way a pin deflates a balloon.

I wish I hadn't already said Yes to the contest. What was I thinking?

In conflicted torment, I search for a topic, or the confidence of belief. As the day approaches, only my characteristic pride prevents me from dropping out. I've also been deeply moved by the recent reading of two other books. *The Last Temptation of Christ*, by Nikos Kazantzakis (1955), and *The Man Nobody Knows*, by Bruce Barton (1925). My own theology is evolving because of such illicit exposures to thinking from outside our bubble of theology.

I now place greater emphasis on God's grace and love than previously. And these two books present to me an intriguing image of a Christ figure whose very humanity is itself an essential component of his identity and mission—for God to know what it is to be human, and then to die on the cross and save us from our sins.

The growth of protests against the draft and our undeclared war in Vietnam, simultaneously with the demonization of returning military, increasingly press into my awareness the hypocrisy of the church and of America in declaring itself to be God's Country. The fire-hot race riots around the country, including an hour's drive away in Detroit, haunt my brain into asking nagging questions about racial inequality and social justice. The turmoil in the world around begins to nest inside of me as well. *I need to believe in Christ, to have God save me from myself and from this frightening world.*

In this state of a grandiose hunger to save the world, I title my speech after the book, *The Man Nobody Knows*. I want to convey a radically new vision, for me at least, of the historical Christ figure.

I walk onto the school auditorium's stage full of fear and adrenaline when my turn comes. I stand at the podium, stunned for a moment, surprised by the number of people in the audience. *God, there are a lot of people here! And the auditorium is huge compared to what I thought it was. I feel small.*

It might have been pride, or perhaps my new vision of Christ, that drives me to reach deep inside for the courage to begin. I remember to find my breath. *This is going to be like announcing to the world my belief in Christ.*

I think this might be the end of what few friendships I have at school. The fact that much of what I am about to say is heresy within my family's religious tradition adds to the storm already living inside. *Dad would be ashamed of me—if he knew. I am scared.*

But I already know from preaching that the only way to get through this fear is to take a deep breath and jump in. Then the rhythm of speaking comes to me. I've also learned the trick of speaking to individuals in the audience, rather than to the crowd. Looking people in the eyes, and so making personal contact with at least a few people, helps reduce my nervousness. I reach for the passion of my faith, as if to bolster it. And then reach deeper yet for the passion and enthusiasm this new image of Christ brings me. I pray to God, as I have for days. *Use me, God, if you want—not for my glory, but for yours.* Then I speak.

I speak of a Christ who rose above daily life, but who did so while intimately knowing life's struggles. He was immersed in a world of death, disease, hypocrisy, and political oppression. Christ was a man who had mysterious relationships with women. They gathered around him like friends. His apostles themselves were jealous of his relationship with one woman in particular, Mary Magdalene, whom I learn even has one of the gnostic gospels attributed to her.

"Why did the Church suppress her writings and teachings of Jesus as she recorded them? Why?" I wonder aloud.

"Mystery surrounds this man, Christ. He was a carpenter, in a time when muscle alone did the work of cutting and hewing timber; the kind of work that makes men sweat, puts calluses on their hands, and muscles in their arms and backs. He was certainly not the pale weakling portrayed in many paintings. The color of his skin was more likely black or olive than white. The pictures we have been offered of an effeminate soft-looking, neutered male are hardly accurate."

"What Christ offers us is a truly radical philosophy of how to live our lives. His ideas, his beliefs, are so radical that were we to adopt them today, the world would change before our very eyes."

"He made no distinction between principles for how to live our personal lives, or how to conduct politics or business. He said, 'Love your enemies...'"

I let silence fill the auditorium to uncomfortableness before I repeat the phrase: "Love your enemies."

I want the profound nature of Jesus's thoughts to fill the air with a sweet rhythm, like dreamy music.

"...whoever slaps you on your right cheek, turn the other to him also" (Matthew 5:39).

"Therefore do not worry about tomorrow, for tomorrow will worry about its own things" (Matthew 6:34).

"Assuredly, I say to you, unless you are converted and become as little children, you will by no means enter the kingdom of heaven" (Matthew 18:3).

"Hypocrite! First remove the plank from your own eye, and then you will see clearly to remove the speck from your brother's eye" (Matthew 7:5).

"So the last will be first, and the first last" (Matthew 20:16).

"And again I say to you, it is easier for a camel to go through the eye of a needle than for a rich man to enter the kingdom of God" (Matthew 19:24).

"Jesus turned water to wine at a wedding party, surely the act of a man with a practical sense of humor and of one who enjoys a good time. This is not the performance of a mere miracle, but the embracement of play, joy, and laughter. Of community."

"He disdained the spiritual materialism and powers of his day. In a rage, he throws the moneylenders out of the temple, hardly the act of a weakling. He knew what it was to be angry, righteously angry. He knew what it was to doubt God, and to suffer."

"When Jesus learned of his friend Lazarus' death, the scriptures say, 'Jesus wept.' Jesus wept!" (John 11:35)

"He cried. This is a man, unlike so many of us today, who was not afraid to cry. This is a man who loved his friends, who cried upon hearing of one's death."

"These are human traits," I say. "It was his humanity, his experience as a human that makes him able to relate to who we are. After all, if his personal failure were not possible, how could he truly understand our struggles? Without an experience of the loneliness that knows the absence of any God, no promise of a sunrise, how could he be capable of interceding on our behalf for all of humanity?"

I picture a Christ figure whose life is a paradoxical blurring of the lines between spiritual ecstasy, human darkness, and childlike wonder.

Time disappears. Then my speech is over, as if I just stumbled into a blind alley. It's over.

I stand there, suddenly self-conscious, with nothing else to say, and look out at a crowd of peers. Silence rules. Awkwardly, looking for an exit line, "Thank you," I say, and turn to walk off the stage. The crowd burst into applause. And then they rise to their feet as if they are one body and give a standing ovation.

I am stunned.

And I am honored. For surely, *I have not done this, but God has used me. Just as I asked him to do in my prayers.* I had not exactly asked God for power, but that is, I suspect now, my heart's hidden desire. I wanted the power to make people notice me, respect me, even like me. *If I can be humble enough, then God will like me too, and use me this way.*

I like the feeling of power as I hold an audience's attention with my words and my presence. It is like a religious formula, a recipe, I suspect. *So long as I can remember that whatever good I do is not me, but God in me, then maybe he will keep using me this way. I pray he will.*

When the time comes for the statewide Speech Contest a few weeks later, I am still praying that God will use me. But I am in agony going into the event. On this day, I have no belief or faith in God.

It is like I lost my identity in a stadium full of people, like my religious passion got up and walked away, disappeared into the milling crowd without me. I search and pray. I pray from as deep a place inside as I know how to reach. But I have no faith this day. It did not come on the wings of a dove, even at the last minute, in response to my prayers. God feels absent to me, as if he withdrew to some distant corner of the universe.

My speech is passionless: dead. I do not even place in the competition.

I am humiliated. I let God down. I betrayed myself, too. Maybe I had too much pride this time, and not enough faith, and that is why God did not use me.

I am an outcast as I walk through the milling crowd of excited kids in the hallway on my way to the bathroom. I know they will all just dismiss me as a Jesus Freak now. The thought of being categorized, and so dismissed, isolates me. My eyes look to no other for friendly comfort. I look to the floor in shame.

I watch myself walk down the lonely hallway to the bathroom door, even as shame wells up within, for my body's needs. *I want to be invisible. I tried to add physicality and humanity to Christ's divinity, but I am still ashamed—of being human.*

An energy comes into my life during this time that saves me, that gives me something to live for besides my faltering faith. She is Lisa, a junior student living in a central Michigan small town a couple of hours north of us. She is everything I am not.

Lisa laughs from her belly with the ease that a meadowlark sings, causing everyone around her to laugh too. She is class president, president of the thespian club, editor of the school newspaper, cheerleader captain, prom queen, and valedictorian of her class. And Lisa is pretty. Right pretty. And she is a member of the church. We meet at a tri-state church youth rally where I am a speaker.

"You can come preach at our church," Lisa says. "My Dad would love it. Sometimes he's the only man and has to do the preaching and song leading and serve the communion too, all by himself."

It is a small church, twenty or thirty people, plus the few tourists, Church of Christ members who drift through town on vacation. The invitation to preach is also an invitation to spend time with Lisa, so I spend a lot of weekends with Lisa and her folks.

I like Lisa a lot. She has long brown hair and brown eyes that open with a softness when she looks at me. And then the electricity sparkles between us.

Her round face lights up like a full moon when she laughs, which she does often. People love being around her, and I get more attention now too, for being her boyfriend.

She is the light of hope in the darkness of my life. She loves me despite my questions. It is me she loves, and I have never felt such open-hearted acceptance before.

Her dad throws me the car keys one Sunday morning and I drive the four of us to church. He sits up front with me in the car and Lisa and her mom are in the back. I stop at the red light. It is a one-stoplight town with wide single lanes leading up to the intersection.

The tourists are in town, and it is a busy Sunday morning. There are three cars in front and another two behind me when I look in the rearview mirror and see a car coming up way too fast behind, weaving around and passing other cars. The car slows, as if hesitating for a moment. Now he's riding the center line of the road, on the edge of possible oncoming traffic, and is positioning to cut in front of all of us, waiting our turn in line so he can jump ahead and be the first one through!

The bastard! I hate people who cut in line, people who take advantage of others just because folks don't stand up and say "No!" And God loves Order.

Righteous rage flushes through me and I think about pulling my car over to the centerline, so he'll have to be completely in the oncoming traffic lane if he goes for it.

I don't. He does.

I look over to shoot arrows of hate and condemnation into the car as it drives by and there, there in the driver's seat, is a white-knuckled young man, the fingers of both hands wrapped around the steering wheel. His eyes are locked on the light and road ahead. Sitting in the passenger seat, but feet from me as he hits the gas pedal in anticipation of the turning of the light, is a pale-faced young woman with eyes wide and mouth open, leaning forward as if to speed up the car. She clutches to her chest a small baby with the bluest of faces—facing me.

The light turns green. He accelerates into the intersection blaring on his horn and makes the left turn with tires screaming toward the hospital before oncoming traffic can even think to move their cars.

He is gone. Silence descends like a thick fog. Traffic begins to move as if nothing had happened. I think I am the only one in the world who even saw it. I am stunned. Compassion floods through me. What was rage is now shame for having ever felt it.

Drive Larry! You are going to church. To preach! Wake up! But all I can feel is a sea of penetrating silence all around me. My mind is stripped of truth, of answers of any kind. I swim in a vast knowing—that I do not know.

I do not know how to live in such an emptiness of identity.

I stand and walk up to the podium to preach, am going to preach about Jesus and the Truth and the Way and—

I try, but I am empty of all the Truth I thought I knew. I am naked.

I stand naked in the pulpit in front of Lisa, her father and mother, sisters and husbands, and a handful of other folks. I stand naked before the invisible altar of self-revelation: *I have been willing to* condemn people to hell for the sake of blind loyalty to my inherited beliefs and theology.

But the raw Truth is, I do not know the Truth.

Is the Bible really from God, in any way? Is there a God? There is no end to such questions once the door is cracked open, even a little to them. No wonder it is a sin to question the Bible.

I stand at the pulpit, receiving a stream of revelations from on high. *My proclaimed religion is an inheritance of theology resting on an unconscious foundation of beliefs and needs. This inheritance is rooted in a frailty of human need for identity, security, specialness, and superiority. Whatever Truth-seeking once lived in this religious legacy is now concretized into an idolatry of theology. There is an innate hunger for truth—but our attempts to own it are destined for failure.*

The arrogance of my own mind disgusts me, believing I possess some privileged standing with God that others do not, as if their integrity and rationality were somehow inferior to mine. I am cut adrift into a turbulent sea of doubt.

What kind of God would place the Truth of our salvation within a context of ambiguity? What conceit lives in me that would believe I have the Truth, and others don't? Am I more sincere? Is my mind brighter? What kind of God, desirous of our salvation, would create such tricky paths for our spiritual navigation?

I vow in my loneliness. *I will be superior to the sheep of inherited revelations sitting in the pews below me.*

I am sick. My stomach turns, and I want to throw up right here from the pulpit. "Jesus loves us. He died for our sins...." I begin to preach, stumbling my way through quoting scriptures. But I cannot get the blue baby's closed eyes out of my eyes.

Lisa's father stands with the hymnal in his left hand and with his right directs the congregation of perhaps twenty folks in singing the invitation song with his deep southern Tennessee accent. In a single song, we affirm God's "Amazing grace..." and our own wretchedness.

This is the ceremonial time for us wretched ones to walk to the front, as I stand before them, encouraging folks to "come forward and be saved or rededicate your life to God."

But there has been no inspired recitation of Truth in my sermon. My preaching on this Sunday inspires no one to come forward and give his or her life anew to God.

No one compliments me afterwards, either. Not even Lisa. That afternoon, she and I make out down at the lake house. For a time, I am not haunted by the closed eyes of Baby Blue.

I like science, chemistry, and biology classes in school, and on my own read about cosmology and evolution, the history of the Bible, and comparative religions. My faith in the Bible, as inspired by God, word-for-word, is crumbling.

I read about the Council of Nicaea, in AD 325. *These men are actually voting on whether Jesus is the Son of God! What? That wasn't always just accepted Christian theology? Oh my God! This is a belief men had to vote on! Is this the book I am betting my faith and life on?*

I stumble upon biblical research on the authorship of the Pentateuch, the first five books of the Old Testament. *We preach Moses wrote them as received from God, but here biblical scholars say there were at least five authors and—*

What am I to believe? What is the Truth? Did God write the Bible or is it a creation of men in service of—who and what?

As surety of my possessing Truth loosens, curiosity demands I research yet more about the origins of the Bible.

My world and life are in an earthquake. We say we possess and preach *the* Truth. Jesus promised, after all, "And you shall know the truth, and the truth shall make you free" (John 8:32).

But I am beginning to suspect we don't really want the Truth. We are happy with ours just the way it is and are not interested in any disruptions to our comfort.

We mock the Pharisees and Sadducees of Jesus' time for auguring about how many angels can sit on the head of a needle, but will God really send human souls to Hell if they don't ever have the chance to even hear the Truth? Might people be better off if they never have the chance to reject Christ? Or will the Southern Baptists suffer in eternal fire and brimstone just for using a piano in their worship services?

I see the faces of kids at school—Joe, Sam, Keith, Chris, Julie—I see them screaming in my nightmares. They stand screaming while fiery sulfur rains down upon them out of the sky. I see them tortured in this Hell, tortured for eternity just because they do not have—have not heard the Truth, believed, confessed their sins and repented, and been baptized by immersion for the forgiveness of their sins.

I am tortured by them. *I do not want to believe in such a God as this.*

I am in dangerous territory. Asking questions. Am I letting my desires shape my beliefs?

I need to believe in God. I want to believe in God. He is my companion. I talk to him every day and cannot imagine life without him walking me to school.

I have to believe in God. I, we, would all live like wild animals without God in our lives. I am a tortured soul already living in Hell.

I again wake in a cold sweat with an aching hard penis and God shaking his finger in my face. Again. And again.

It's not easy for Mom and Dad when I ask to borrow the car one Friday so I can attend a Muslim worship service at a mosque in Detroit. They didn't mind too much when, out of curiosity, I attended the worship services of other Christian churches, like the Baptists and Methodists. However, my desire to attend the Islamic Mosque resulted in a fight. Dad and I often find ourselves engaged in heated religious arguments. Dad asks why I want to go.

"'Cause I'm searching for Truth. If we have it, then what are you afraid of?"

"I'm not afraid. I have my faith in God and in Christ. I believe the Bible is from God."

In such arguments, I now often aggressively cut Dad off before he can even finish his sentence. He does the same to me, but I already know how he will answer my questions.

"Are you afraid I might find out the Muslims have the Truth?"

"No."

"Have you ever studied Islam? Or Buddhism, or Hinduism?"

"No. I—"

"Then how can you say you have the Truth?"

"Because Christ rose from the dead. That's proof he was God's Son. I choose to have faith in him. Mohammed and Buddha, neither of them rose from the dead. Did they?"

"No, but Buddha was born out of his mother's side, and *he* came out talking. That ought to account for something. Investigation at least."

Dad laughs at the silliness of taking seriously a talking baby being born out of a woman's side. Who could ever compare such a primitive pagan myth to the virgin-born Christ dying on the cross for our sins and then rising from the dead?

"And Mohammed didn't have to return from the dead," I continue. "He left his proof that he was God's prophet right here, on earth. It's like this everlasting miracle that people can still touch today if they want. You say Christ rose from the dead, but you choose to believe it on faith."

"Well, there is no other reasonable explanation for why his disciples would be willing to risk their lives."

Now we cut each other off, and our voices rise in competition for a listener.

"Do you even know what Mohammed's miracle, his proof, is?" I ask.

"No, but—"

"It's the Koran. Mohammed was an uneducated camel driver who spent his time hanging out in this mountain cave, talking to God. Then, one day, people started writing down what God was telling him, and that's how we have the Koran. He was a completely uneducated man. Yet he authored what the Muslims claim is the most beautiful piece of Arabic literature ever written. That's his everlasting miracle. That's what they claim, anyway. And that's why I want to go check them out."

Mother has been present the entire time, standing off to the side and out of the line of fire. She is clearly agitated because she doesn't like us raising our voices. She had begun first to pace, then to wring her hands together. Finally, to use a phrase she herself often used in instruction to us, her children, she can no longer "bite her tongue."

Speaking of her faith in God and Christ, she says: "I don't care if it's true or not. I'm going to believe it, anyway! That's what faith is!

Life is not worth living without God."

Mom's simple honesty empties my lungs of air and ends the argument. There is no fighting against a faith of such clarity. She said what Dad could not, and in doing so she gave me that day a great gift, even as I then took it as a curse upon my life. My soul also cursed each of them for the hypocrisy I perceived in them.

And Mom outright saying that my life is not worth living without God. Without their God, to be specific. I am trapped!

I had always known this in some way; it is an understood Truth we live with. But to say, "I don't care if it's true or not. I am going to believe it anyway!" Surely, this is an eruption of heresy spoken in a moment of Truth, with a capital T. This dropping of any pretension of rationality—this reliance upon blind Faith.

I attend Michigan Christian Junior College, now Rochester Christian University, to help me in my search for the Truth. Studying the Bible with a real professor, a doctor of theology, excites me. *Surely, he will have the answers I seek.*

Other students seem to attend our three-days-a-week Bible Class like it is any other class. *They listen politely and accept whatever formulistic lessons the professor has prepared for us. It's routine. It's a ritual. And except for me, absent is any sense of a quest or serious search for Truth.*

And so, I stand out in class, awkwardly asking my damn questions. I do not even remember the question I asked on this day. Perhaps it is something about the two conflicting creation stories in Genesis. Maybe about how to know when to read the Bible literally, and when not to, such as when the Bible says "the sun stood still" when the Israelites marched around the walls of Jericho to make them fall. Perhaps it is one involving the meaning of a word in the original language or something to do with contradictions involving differing versions of manuscript fragments relied upon for translation. Dr. Bible stammers around a bit, searching for an answer, and then, "Larry, would you come by my office after class?"

I am excited. I've never been to a professor's office before. *Maybe he's going to commend me for my sincerity and perceptiveness of thinking or something.* I knock and he opens the door for me to come in. But he does not ask me to sit down. Instead, he simply closes the door behind me.

His office looks just like Dad's office at church. There is the requisite desk and then three walls lined with scholarly religious books from floor to ceiling. I recognize some by their jacket covers and lust to look through this collection of knowledge and wisdom.

But now Dr. Bible half looks me in the eye and says, "Larry, I need to ask a favor of you. I need you to stop asking questions in class. You are causing me to question my faith."

My head swirls and I feel dizzy. *I thought I was to be complimented on my search for Truth,* but his words echo off the inside walls of my skull, without escape.

"I need you to stop asking questions. You are causing me to question my faith!" What the...?

And that was it. Dr. Bible opens his office door and I walk out in a stupor, not believing what I've heard or what he said.

I confess to some strange mixtures of pride stirred in with some fierce anger, and a bit of shame thrown in for spice. Pride, that I have such powers as to make this diploma-attaining man of God question his faith and a fierce anger at the absolute hypocrisy of his claims to Truth. My face burns red with the shame of walking alone in the world. The shame of one not being able to trust or even know who I am?

But how am I ever to trust my own mind?

I Am So Lonely

Excuse me please but
have you by any chance
seen my Belonging lying around anywhere?

I'm pretty sure I came in with it.
I mean, hummingbird has hers.
Horned toad has his.
Antelope and butterfly and coyote have theirs.
All the other creatures—theirs too.
Even trees and the grasses have roots
for knowing their place in the world.

And I am surely better than... superior to them
cause God after all did give me a soul,
but not one to them.
I am more intelligent, have better hands and
build the best of walls and truly have
the cream of skin colors
plus the one true religion so...
might you have seen my Belonging anywhere?

I am so lonely and in despair without it.
Nor can I find *Here* either.
Might you please be able to tell me
where I am by any chance?

Wild Joy

I seem to have lost my way
and this map I carry
is not taking me to the joy and peace I desire.
I grow weary and fill with rage
trying to change the landscape to fit it.

Perhaps my beliefs—are not strong enough
my prayers—not fervent enough
my enemies—not hated enough.
I will not be a fool. I shall try harder.

Chapter 5

LOST

It is during my senior year of high school that the damn questions begin to haunt my days and nights and undermine my faith in the revealed God and religion of my parents. But it is in the Christian Colleges where I develop a fearsome and self-righteous loathing for the utter hypocrisy of those who passionately claim to possess the Truth, yet who also lack any interest or will for an active search of the same.

I transfer to Oklahoma Christian College (now Oklahoma Christian University) the following year, after my encounter with Dr. Bible. *Surely there, at a four-year college, surely, they will be seriously searching for the treasure of sacred Truth.* My disappointment is immense.

I double major, in Bible and a pre-professional Social Work track that includes classes in psychology, sociology, and anthropology. I have Bible classes three days a week there, for three years. Each class begins with the ritual of a prayer. "Oh Lord God, help us to open our hearts and minds to thy word, and to so receive thy truth and be free."

Then the download affirming that we are the one true church begins, selectively choosing chapter and verse here and there, like picking ripe peaches from a tree.

The Dr. Bibles selectively pick the story and verse illustrating how to interpret properly the word of God through a literal understanding and interpretation of the holy scriptures.

And where the Dr. Bibles see Truth, I see theological indoctrination. Where they see God's word inscribed onto paper, I see the insertion of perceptional viruses into the minds of my peers.

I also cannot help but remember the stories from my youth of how my Great Grandpa Smith, Mom's grandpa, helped start Lockney Christian College, in Texas, in 1894. Each morning, the Christian education there started with a woman supervising the young ladies in their long skirts alight from their buckboards. "And if even so much as an ankle showed, they got sent home."

Of course, in those days, it was proper to put bloomers on piano legs too! Apparently, us men are just prone to being tempted by the slightest suggestion. But it all leaves me scratching my head when morality and Truth also seem to change with convenience and the times we live in.

Such considerations leave me judgmentally thinking of the school administration. *They are more interested in measuring the length of the girls' skirts, to be sure they are no more than an inch above the knee than they are in searching for God's Truth! They care more about policing student behaviors, making sure there's no smoking or drinking or dancing going on, than asking when to read the Bible literally and when not to!*

I think, too, of how mixed swimming was a sin when we lived in the dry plains of Colorado. But when we move to Michigan, *The Land of Lakes*, with water everywhere, Dad explains the change in theology, saying, "It's different here. People live on lakes and have boats and..."

And I scratch my head. But I like seeing the girls in their bathing suits!

I learn more about religion in my psychology classes than I do in any of my three remaining years of Bible classes. It seems the professors of the two disciplines never talk with each other. *Is this a kind of socialized schizophrenia*, I wonder. It's like the mind gets compartmentalized and fragmented and doesn't see the inherent, uncomfortable discrepancies between various beliefs or knowledge sets.

Like when we study psychological defense mechanisms and how people find confirmation for their beliefs, even in circumstances that ought to challenge them. Like when a cult leader predicts a date for the return of Christ, the rapture, and end of the world. People even sell their homes to prepare for their ascension. And yet, when Christ doesn't descend from the clouds as predicted—"Well, it's because we, the faithful, showed up and obeyed the commands from God to prepare, and so we saved the world."

Sociology class is where I discover Eric Hoffer's *The True Believer: Thoughts on the Nature of Mass Movements* (Hoffer 1951). He was a longshoreman and social philosopher who studied and wrote about the conditions and ideas that lead individuals and groups into religious and political movements of extremism and fanaticism, such as authoritarianism and fascism. True Believers are also often so identified with and moved by emotional fears or physical insufficiencies that facts themselves are irrelevant. It's simply easier to inhabit a worldview of us against them, of good against evil, than one of subtility, ambiguity, and co-creative responsibility.

That's what the Church of Christ people are, I think. *They are True Believers.*

And what makes our intellectual integrity any greater than those who have opposing theologies? There is no application here of reflection or insight into our own claims of exclusive possession of the Truth!

Whether political or religious, Eric Hoffer notes a propensity for adherents to hold fanatical beliefs with a mental dogmatic absolutism that is hinged on emotional resonance rather than facts.

It is a paradoxically long and short distance from theologically seeing the world as dangerously evil to perceiving psychological normalcy as pathologically insane. I make the leap.

They can see the hypocrisy in others, I think, *but not in themselves! It's like people use their minds to justify what their emotional selves need to believe in! People are like unconscious sheep. I want to be different! I'm not going to be like them,* I proclaim internally with my harsh righteousness. *I want Truth, and its promised freedom.*

It would be interesting to know how many people remember their first drink. How many people, I wonder, remember this event, say, compared to their first kiss, first sex, or first car? My first beer stands out to me as a junction in life, like the opening words of Robert Frost's poem, *The Road Not Taken*.

The folks warned me, of course, that would be true, that one drink of the evil spirits might be enough to send a person down the road to hell. But with the substantial risk of drinking my first beer, it becomes impossible for me to accept my parent's belief that alcohol is pure evil. At this life junction, my parents lose additional credibility as speakers of truth. And I step onto a forbidden path and into a dangerous relationship with alcohol.

Lisa's older sister, Julie, recently married Paul, a tall, slender, red-haired, and freckled guy who was a year or two older than me. Paul has a mischievous humor and is quick to laugh. I imagine Paul being the clown in any group he is part of. I like Paul, and we have a growing friendship, the likes of which are yet new to me.

Once, while I was napping in the bedroom, Paul rearranged the furniture in my living room just to see what kind of rise he could get out of me upon waking. We have fun together. Paul joins the army and is stationed at Fort Sill for a brief time. He later went from there to Vietnam and came back a different man, one unreachable by me. But before that, when we all lived in Oklahoma, Lisa and I eagerly visited him and Julie.

On this life-changing day, after the initial energy of sisters hugging and Paul and my backslapping reunion, he and I were off to buy some spark plugs for his car. Returning to the apartment, we decide it is too miserably hot and humid out to stand in the sun and change the plugs in his car.

"Let's go inside where it's cool," Paul says.

"Great idea," I respond.

As the four of us gather around the small, square dining table next to the refrigerator, Paul asks, "What do you want to drink, Larry? I'm having a beer."

Julie is getting cokes for herself and Lisa. My mind is replaying all the times I heard Dad preach against the evils of alcohol. "Who among us would get on an airplane if we knew, say, ten percent of the seats were going to drop out of the plane during the flight? You never know ahead, but what if you might be one of those ten percent who will just turn into an alcoholic on your first drink? Quick as that, your life could be ruined."

Oklahoma Christian would kick me out of school if they knew I had a beer. Just like they do to people for dancing too,

All this contributes to my uncomfortable hesitation before answering. Then, like a rubber band stretched too far, the weight of feeling lied to about God, and country, and the weight of life as a social outcast is more than I care to any longer bear. Something snaps inside me.

"I'll have a beer too, Paul." I try to say this like I've said it maybe hundreds of times before.

Immediately, a Rocky Mountain Coors is on the table in front of me. Bringing the can to my lips, I wonder if I am about to make the physical transformation into an alley-living drunk. I can almost see myself as a dirty and smelly wino lying in some gutter.

The beer's taste is unlike anything I've had before, but the second and third swallows go down real easy. And it's cold. Before the can is empty, I like the taste. I'm also feeling happy, like I am finally one of the guys.

So, this is what real people do, I think to myself. *This is what it's like to sit at a table with people and feel comfortable. To feel relaxed! To tell stories and laugh! I've never felt this socially at ease before. I feel like I belong*. It is a religious experience for me.

"I'll have another one too, Paul."

Much later in life, I come to recognize a spiritual aspect, a spiritual hunger, to the pattern I develop of excessive drinking. It is the nature of many things in life to serve us for a time, but if not boundaried, to become our master rather than our servant. In the way that religion, power, money, politics, work, cars, food, or even exercise can be used to numb an empty hunger inside, I begin to use alcohol and drugs for just this purpose. And so it is that I respond to my parent's beliefs and fears about alcohol, the shadow of their guiding hand on my shoulder.

I took anthropology classes nearby at what is now the University of Central Oklahoma because Oklahoma Christian University was too small to offer such. There, I was introduced to the writings of the renowned anthropologist, Dr. Edward T. Hall, including his books, *The Hidden Dimension* and *The Silent Language*.

Regarding the later book, the famous psychologist Erich Fromm wrote, "*The Silent Language* shows how cultural factors influence the individual behind his back, without his knowledge." (Hall 1959) This unconscious shaping of the human psychic obsesses me. *How am I ever to be the author of my life if authorship remains hidden in my unconscious mind?*

Reading Ned, as Dr. Hall was known by friends and as I came to know and love him dearly forty years later, was like being a kid and discovering a hidden light switch in a dark and unfamiliar closet, wherein one just knows a valuable treasure is stored. His books open me to exploring how my fundamental experiences of the world, such as even concepts of time and space, and interpretations of body language, are essentially and mysteriously shaped by the culture I live in, and that reciprocally lives inside me.

He introduces me to culture as a kind of atmospheric influence that is difficult to even be aware of, except through the self's exposure to contrasting foreign or unfamiliar environments. *God, not only do I need to be conscious of how my parents' religious and political views shape my life, but now I need to become aware of culture as a shadowy shaper of my life too. If I can choose versus inherit my religious and political views, through attention and self-awareness, perhaps I can also influence culture's impacts on my perceptions of life and self as well.*

Ned was eighty-three years old as we got to know each other better over lunch at the La Posada Hotel in Santa Fe, NM, where we became acquainted. He is still a vibrant man of ideas, filled with a passion for exploring and understanding culture. He is a man of international professional stature and contribution, being honored with the Anthropology in Media Award (former recipients include Stephen Jay Gould, Jane Goodall, and Tony Hillerman). He's also just finished teaching a doctorate-level graduate class at the University of New Mexico.

Ned's life is that of a provocateur, a revealer of people to themselves. He's spent his life exploring how culture unconsciously shapes our everyday perspectives on life, and how it determines our behaviors, in families, schools, business, and government. With six books to his name, he told me, "I have another six I'd like to write."

But he knows his time is limited, so he is presently focusing on the issue he believes is most vital for him to share about and speak to. "My current work is about pain," he says. "Human pain, and our strategies for coping with it."

Ned is white-haired now. The lines on his face reflect his early years spent outdoors in southwest deserts and mountains. Working on the Navajo and Hopi reservations in the 1930s and 1940s gave him stories he still loves to tell. It gifted him not only friendships but some of his early learning in human culture. He is a man who has loved horses, dogs, and critters all his life. His weathered face reveals a continuing love of spending time outside. The same facial lines converge with the ones that come with his characteristic quick smile and love of life.

We sit in the southwestern-styled dining room with a high viga ceiling and a kiva-style fireplace in the corner, settle in next to the windows, and look out onto the patio, where we would be if the weather were warmer. Ned is dressed in casual slacks and his comfortably worn tweed sport coat, ever the professor. We finish our food. I am enjoying my coffee and Ned sips his tea.

"I gave a talk recently to a group of teenagers at the Exploratorium. It's an integrative art and science museum in San Francisco. They were a noisy bunch of kids. Nobody could get them quieted down. Well! I started right off by saying, 'Life is painful.' I had their attention right away. People don't like to talk about it. But it is! I'm writing a book about pain, you know. There are basically three ways people deal with chronic pain. Three strategies."

"When my wife was sick, she was in severe chronic pain. I read this book, *How to Cope with Chronic Pain*. It's about physical pain. But it got me thinking about other kinds of pain. Like chronic emotional and cognitive pain. I used to have a dog that every time I went for a walk, well if I didn't take her, she'd start crying. She'd really be hurt. Even animals can feel emotional pain."

"One way people deal with chronic pain is by turning it out against the world. Literally, they use their pain like a weapon and take it out on others. These are people who go through life using and hurting other people, using their anger, manipulation, and aggression. Usually, they don't even know they're doing this."

"The second strategy is to turn it in upon yourself. To become depressed, or alcoholic, or a drug addict. Or a workaholic and a high achiever. But they literally become self-destructive in some way."

"When people think of pain, they tend to think of physical pain. But emotional pain is equally real. Look at the Indians. The Blacks. That's what they're struggling with as populations. Tremendous burdens of generational chronic emotional pain. Old historical stuff. And a lot of it is current too."

"Racism causes tremendous pain. When I was teaching, I used to tell my classes this. Students would sometimes tell me they finally understood the pain they were in. They hadn't been able to understand why they were in pain."

"The thing about emotional pain like this is it's not like a broken arm. There, you have a visible reason for your pain. But that doesn't make the emotional pain any less real."

"The third strategy is one of transformation. These people turn their experience into a positive resource to draw upon, like creativity. The person literally uses the pain to become someone else. Some artists manage to do this. And people who use the energy of their pain to help people in the world around them. They identify with other people in pain. It's not that they don't feel their pain anymore. They just don't identify with it in a way that makes them want to hurt others, or themselves. They learn to use it."

While talking, Ned places his elbows on the table and cradles his cheeks and face in his hands. It's a habit he displays sometimes when thinking, as if going into a trance when talking about material that he's thought deeply about, and cares about. His eyes occasionally go far away for a moment, unfocused and into the distance, as though seeing something others cannot. But now, he rubs his cheeks vigorously a couple of times, as though to bring himself back to the sensory world. He fixes his blue eyes and looks directly into mine.

"So," Ned exclaims, in the way he has of making the word an exclamatory sentence. "Tell me. What's your story? How have you handled pain in your life?"

Navigating my parent's chagrin and pain, I find myself in graduate school at a liberal, ungodly state school where the temptations of the Devil run wild—the University of Oklahoma. Lisa and I marry the summer before my junior year of college and together we make the move to Norman, OK. Lisa is the harbor in my life who gives me shelter amidst my loss of faith, first in the Church, then in the Bible, then in God, and in my capacity to know any objective and ultimate Truth.

Graduate school increases the stresses and challenges of life. As my parents feared, I am unprepared for the easy access to the forbidden fruits of drugs and sex. It is now 1971 and the release of the *Pentagon Papers* reveals political lies, deceit, and even war in service of sequential Presidents sustaining personal power. Complete loss of faith in the integrity of government is executed for me with President Gerald Ford's pardon of former President Nixon, whom I thought should be tried as an international war criminal.

Students protesting Nixon's expansion of the war into Cambodia resulted in the Kent State Massacre (1970), killing four and injuring nine unarmed people, and the rise of women's liberation in the same era, provide a brief context for the social unrest of the times and my inner disorientation, I take my first psychedelic drug, mescaline, and nothing is the same afterwards. I sit under a large shady tree in the park as the world takes on vibrant colors and waves of emotion wash through me. Energy fields of people and trees become visible. The world is not what I thought it was, nor am I who I thought.

Increasingly, I want to feel part of the world that I have always been forbidden to partake of. I hunger for belonging. I hunger for some of that free love now set loose upon the land.

I'm climbing onto my motorcycle after class one day when Tina, a pretty, petite blond classmate, fond of wearing miniskirts, asks me for a ride home. She invites me in and proceeds to change out of her miniskirt and blouse into short shorts and tee-shirt right in front of me. We are soon laying on her bed and kissing and making out when she asks, "Aren't you married?"

"Yeah, but I want you."

The clothes are quickly off and we are crawling under the covers and there I am about to commit adultery—betray Lisa, even though she is the ground of being in my life. I hunger to claim this body as my own. I yearn to experience the pleasures and liberation that it screams for, having shed the believer in me. And there, as the animal in me rises to meet the animal in Tina, I feel I am partaking of a Holy Sacrament. It is the righteous reclaiming of bodily pleasures away from their declaration as evil. As not to be trusted.

If this is evil, God, then so be it. You can send me to hell for this if you will, but I see no evil in two people sharing such pleasure and ecstasy as this. I refuse to believe my body and its desires are evil. And I am lost in the fiery heat of the rut. Later, of course, I live in hell. Trying to sort out my relationship with Lisa and the hunger for more of the uninhibited passion discovered in the bed of another woman. And then more women.

I recognize myself as akin to Pavlov's dog, only I'm conditioned to see the naked skin of females as forbidden fruit, and now I swim in the hormonal stew of young adulthood and the loss of an orienting belief system and young horny women everywhere.

I thought it was just guys who wanted sex so much, but again, my world turns upside down. *They want it as much as I do!* Where is a damn reliable script or *Map of Morals and Life* when I need it?

Lisa and I split and get back together, and split again, and then moved back to Michigan together.

The job I take as a school social worker proves to be a comfortable holding ground for folks looking for gentle retirements, while I want to foment a revolution of learning in school systems I see as indoctrination centers. I take more drugs and have more affairs. No girlfriend of Lisa's is off-limits to me.

It's Sunday evening, so of course I think of the folks attending worship services just as Lisa and I decide to party. I load the bong with opiated marijuana, turn on the black lights and the Moody Blues, open the Boones Farm wine, and take a hit of acid. Somewhere, in the fog of all this, with *Nights in White Satin* playing, I look over at Lisa, sitting cross-legged across from me on the floor, and her color is blue. Then her body just melts like candle wax onto the floor.

My Red Cross First Aid college class training kicks in from the deep recesses of my being and I try to give her mouth-to-mouth resuscitation. But no air will go in. *Larry, open her mouth better. Tilt her head more. Look for her tongue. Damn, she's swallowed it! There, now try again.*

Lisa quickly revives and I know, from within my deepest being, that I must leave her for good. *I am killing her through her love and loyalty to me. It is one thing for me to go on my wild search for meaning in life, but I cannot, will not, allow this friend and woman I love so dearly to come with me. No.*

It is a separation and a divorce that nearly kill me.

Wiping Love off the Mirror

Woke in the night
to the ancient voice
of denigration and unworthiness
to never-can and never-will
be enough for the self-love
of relaxing into "just as I am."

Caught the vocal little bugger
in the act of repeating his mantras
as though he owns my ears and heart
"You are not enough...
man enough or good enough
Look at what you didn't complete
yesterday or in your life
Look at all the projects...
You never finish what you start!"

That's when I see Perfectionism
clearly enough to grab hold of the parasitic sucker
and so I hold tight despite
resilient sinewy winding convolutions
of justifications and accusations
of truths and partials until I perceive

How even my truth-telling to self
so easily becomes yet more self-critiquing
through humiliation and belittlement
just more strategies for flagellation
of what is already whole.

Chapter 6

SAVED BY A BEAR—
RE-STORYING THE SACRED

I am ostracized. Outcast. Condemned by God, family, and old church friends. I am a sinner of the worst kind. The Bible says so. "For it would have been better for them not to have known the way of righteousness, than having known *it,* to turn from the holy commandment delivered to them" (2 Peter 2:21).

I am that kind of sinner, the worst kind. The innately flawed kind. A sinner by choice. I throw away the map of reality I inherited from the folks and, in my search for identity and orientation, I fall to what I do know. I know I love women. And sex. And I know drinking and smoking pot too takes away the pain—for a time, anyway. I am the man, now in my mid-twenties, my parents warned me not to become.

I have sex at every opportunity with any woman who will join me. It is a declaration of the innate goodness of the flesh and a proclamation of freedom from a tyrannical religion and God.

I take the most beautiful woman I know, and with my rebellious hunger for the flesh of others, I break her heart dry of love for me. I cannot forgive myself for this except when in the fire of rubbing naked flesh against the nakedness of another. In that flame, in that heat, the animal in me is free of condemnation and judgment.

I am, for the flame's duration, simply free to be—right and pure and in communion with life. It is easy until we put our clothes back on and any needs for emotional intimacy arise. I go through women like a man looking for his familiar coat in new clothing stores.

I take a job as a family therapist/social worker in a runaway shelter for teens in the inner city of Detroit. I'm drawn to the organization because we work as a collective, rather than as a hierarchical organization. It's an idealistic era and we're experimenting with new social structures. It is a baptism for me to work with strong women with feminist orientations.

The subjugation of women to men, which is part of my fundamentalist Christian upbringing, feels just wrong to me. Yet I feel my conditioning is still actively at play. Part of my attraction to the organization is the collective commitment to personal growth, to support the discovery and dismantling of toxic hierarchical social structures that still drive our individual and work lives, like shadows living unseen within.

I am in so much pain, however, that I work ten to twelve hours a day and come back to my little apartment and drink and smoke myself to sleep. I think about suicide a lot. Death seems but an invitation to stop feeling the pain of loneliness, of Mom and Dad's shame of me, and of my own shame for damn near killing Lisa with my drinking and drugs.

I am shame—for just being alive! For just breathing, okay? God Damn it! I'm not supposed to be alive! There is something wrong with me. I'm flawed. *Fucked up, alright? The story I'm supposed to live is dying as a drug addict and alcoholic in a gutter on some anonymous dark street. That, or commit suicide. Either one confirms their worldview; my life is not worth living without God, without Jehovah, who, after all, does love his vengeance.*

Living in the inner city of Detroit as a blond, blue-eyed country boy is an invitation for me to become a conscious student of fear. I witness the fears that rise in me. Fears that, over time, begin to reveal the shadows of my own racial prejudices. I notice how I walk into a room full of people and gravitate initially to the white-skinned folks. I take notice of how I am drawn to the familiar.

I cannot help but remember the road sign on the outskirts of Canyon, TX, that always caught my eye when we visited Mom's folks there. It's what was known as a "sundown sign", and read, in effect, "No black people in town after dark." But it used an overt racial slur rather than the word *black*.

Like with the subjugation of women to the man of the house, as I invite in their awareness, the *us and them* divisions of racial superiority and dominance, mapped into my subconscious, begin to show themselves in my fears and discomforts. I became more attuned to seeing *fear* in others too.

Working in the runaway shelter, I learn to smell degrees and kinds of fear in the kids that come in off the street, and in their families. And I come to see fear both as an informant and, at other times, as an inner parasite or even a predator. In the latter roles, it inspired irrational and destructive behaviors. Like in the woman, a friend of my housemate David, who called our house at two o'clock one morning.

"I need help," she says between sobs and tears. "Please come. I need to leave him. Please... Come get me before he gets back."

David, with a resigned sigh, tells me the boyfriend has a habit of beating her up. We drive over and find her sitting in the city's near darkness on the concrete steps of the apartment building. Sobbing. She's holding her head in her hands and a bag in her lap. One of her eyes seems freshly black and blue. Bruises are on both arms and the cheek opposite her black eye.

"Come on, let's go," we say.

I'm feeling my body on alert, feeling my own fears of some unknown guy driving up and getting violent.

"Come on, let's go," we repeat with an urgency of our own.

"I can't," she says. "I have to stay. At least I know he loves me," she says between sobs. "Else he wouldn't hit me."

We leave her sitting where we found her. I find myself thinking, *this is how Christians are with God. They can't leave their abusive Hell-threatening God because at least he loves them, or else he wouldn't have sent his only son to save them.*

Then I remember a saying picked up somewhere: "Fear the man who's afraid of you."

But what if we only try to hurt what we fear? Could God be afraid of humankind? Kicked us out of the garden, "lest he put out his hand and take also of the tree of life, and eat, and live forever" (Genesis 3: 22).

It's like... like fear can twist our idea of love into something unrecognizable and sometimes even gruesome. You're frigging crazy, Larry! Nobody thinks like this but you!

I cannot help but wonder what a tangled mess and forbidden territory my mind is taking me into.

It is such curiosity and fear that moves me to study my relationship with the people of the night. Some feel like potential predators who hang with the shadows, fleeing even the light of the moon. I feel their probing eyes as they watch the streets for opportunity. I respect them and dislike my fear. With time, though, I notice they walk with a gate that suggests they own the territory. I imitate their simple rhythm that says, "I'm not looking for or taking any trouble. I'm not a victim. If you're looking for a victim, you won't even notice me. I belong."

That helps when walking to the liquor store late at night, or in and out of the bars. Like them, I try to walk as if I own the ground I walk on.

I like Sarah. A lot. She's a bare five-foot tall, eighteen-year-old feminist beauty, recently started volunteering at the Runaway Shelter. For me, there is instant love and lust. I want her.

She has long black hair that falls to her butt like a waterfall. The dancer in her shows when she walks, and her midnight black eyes swallow me whole when they do not turn away from my gaze.

Sarah is my first effort at a relationship after separation from Lisa. However, I still feel the need to try on relationships with as wide a variety of women as possible. It is like shopping around, trying to find what I like and don't like in a woman. I dream there is *one* out there with whom I'd never have conflict. Meanwhile, Sarah and I develop a stormy, intense, and brief relationship.

I find myself caring deeply for Sarah. But I don't have room inside for emotional risk. I don't even know how to enter this masculine forbidden territory of emotional vulnerability, especially when it involves conflict. This does not make me a suitable partner for a relationship. Lisa will be yet many years in the past before I again utter the words, "I love you," to a woman. Still, I want to say these words to Sarah. But they stick in my throat when I think of saying them.

Sarah is also a voracious reader and turns me on to *The Diary of Anais Nin* (Nin 1966), and then Sylvia Plath's poetry and her novel, *The Bell Jar* (Plath 1962). I am inspired by both women and their willingness to walk into forbidden territories of self-inquiry and revelation. Then, upon discovering Carl Jung's, *Memories, Dreams,*

Reflections, I explore my own inner life in deeper ways with a journal of my dreams, experiences, and reflections. The practice becomes lifesaving and serves me to this day (Jung 1963).

"Let's take a canoe trip together," I propose. "In Canada, in Algonquin Provincial Park. I've always wanted to do something like this, and we can rent a canoe there, I hear and...," and I am excited. How good can it get? Canoeing in a wilderness area with my new love.

Nature, going into nature for hikes and camp-outs, is increasingly my solace. My body relaxes somehow when I am outside, and I spend as much time out among the trees and in the forests as I can. I am discovering a game trail, with nature as teacher and healer, that leads me back into a sense and experience of wholeness, of simple belonging.

The trees, rocks, butterflies, birds, and deer—they do not judge me. I appreciate them for this. *People. I am afraid of people. They kill your spirit for the pleasure of a laugh if you let them, or to avoid looking in the mirror of their own beliefs.*

People are but sheep on two legs, and they think they are better than all of nature. Give me some forest and wild rivers. Let's get out of this city!

It is our fourth night out and we camp at the edge of a lake of stillness. In the silent dawn hour before sunrise, the cooking pots and pans bang and clang together loudly and unexpectedly. *What in the world?*

I'm thinking *bear* because I'm a good ex-Boy Scout, and had hung the food by a rope high in a tree before going to bed and cleaned the pots and pans down at the lake and set our tent up a good distance away from the fire pit, where we cooked. I slide myself up to where I can quietly unzip the door of the tent and look out.

"Sarah, it's a bear!" I say in a whisper that is really an excited yell. Now Sarah and I are sneaking our peak out the tent's open door. I've never been this close to a bear in the wild before and I'm as happy as a camper can get and then—

Then the bear looks up. *Our* way. *At us.* Starts walking toward us. It's not supposed to happen this way!

Sarah and I slide back into the tent. I think for a moment about jumping out of the tent, naked as I am, and waving my arms and yelling. I look for something inside the tent to make a noise with— nothing. *Shit! No food in here, though. That's good.*

We feel the bear getting closer. Sarah looks at me with her full-moon dark eyes and I reach for my black-handled Buck hunting knife.

I free the five-inch steel blade from its leather sheath. "Take this," I whisper and pass the knife to Sarah, handle first. I mimic how she can cut her way out, if need be, realizing we are now inside a burrito.

I mean, it is one thing to fight a bear, but it's another to fight a bear when you are all wrapped up inside a blue nylon tent.

I am a good student of fear by now, however, and I feel mine about to jump right out of my chest and throat.

Stop, Larry! This inner voice claims my attention like the hand waving of an old friend interested only in my survival. *Fear is the enemy here. My enemy. Our enemy.*

I remember childhood days of dogs and horses smelling fear on me. And I've smelled its presence on people.

Fight the fear, Larry. Breathe. Get quiet inside. Breathe slowly. Fight the fear. There's no food in here. The bear is only looking for easy food.

Memory flashes me back to the magical evening of last night, as I sat at the lake's edge before crawling into the tent for the night: listening to loon calls drift over quiet waters reflecting sunset colors of oranges, pinks, and reds in the high cirrus clouds overhead and reading favorite passages from the book, *Black Elk Speaks* (Neihardt 1961, 43).

His writing awakens and inspires the eyes of spirit within to open, through which to perceive the world, as if sensing through eyes of wholeness rather than eyes of fragmentation and separation. I inhale with gratitude and wonder the peaceful setting as gentle lake waves lap the rock I am on and am transported into a sense of relationship with all of Life.

"I was seeing in a sacred manner the shapes of all things in the spirit, and the shape of all things as they must live together, like one being." (Neihardt 1972)

I watch the sun drop below the forest green horizon as light dances a rainbow-colors game of continuous change over the lake; quiet waves rhythmically lap at the shore, as if playing orchestral sounds and sensations. Light fades toward darkness and the last primeval call of loons float up off the glassy water and hang there in silence.

Suddenly, the presence of Aunt Eudene is with me. She is Dad's youngest sister. I see her face in a cloud and feel her goodbye. *She's done it. Taken her life. Somehow, I just know it. I feel it.*

Our last conversation together plays over and over inside my skull. We were fond of each other, having before secretly shared our religious doubts and suicidal thoughts. "I don't want to believe in that God anymore, Larry," she confided.

Her suicide is a simple fact to me. I hold no grudge. I know I may yet do the same someday, and I feel at peace with my own death, however it may come.

Time. Space. Here. Now. There. Then. They all blend into this cross-legged sitting at the front door of the tent. This space shrinks to the entirety of the universe.

All my senses are wide-open and alert, and I sit at the circle of the sacred hoop in the center of the universe. There is nowhere else. I sit just inside the tent doorway with my legs crossed and focus my mind on breathing. Slow. Deep. Calm. It requires effort to keep my mind from racing wildly, but desperation pulls me back to this breath. This breath. This breath only...

Conscious breathing, yoga, and meditation have recently come into my life, not as disciplines yet, but as curiosities of interest. This seed of interest screams to me. *NOW—is the time to sink into and follow your breath, Larry, as you never have before. Any panic on our part, any unnecessary startling of the bear, feels to me an invitation for confrontation, or to be perceived as prey.*

The bear is close. We feel her presence. She is here!

She closes the last few yards, and we anticipate the soft but near-silent placement of each paw on the forest floor of pine needles. We can see nothing outside our blue womb of nylon fabric. Sarah and I lock eyes for support. An instinctual acuity of hearing and sensing unveils before us the curtains of the primordial world we sit within. There is nothing between the bear and us.

She is here, standing at the right front corner of the tent. She inhales in a repeated series of audible short and rapid sniffs, then follows these with a louder forceful blowing out of breath through her nostrils. Sniff, sniff, sniffing in, blowing it out. Sniff, sniff, sniffing in, blowing out. Her curiosity investigates us first at ground level, and now from above our heads near the top of the tent. She makes her way, patiently it seems to me, to the back of the tent, sniffing us high and low, as she goes around onto the left side of the tent and now to the front left corner. Sniffing loudly. Our heads turn on our necks like a couple of owls as we track her progression and attempt to hold on to calm, to make no noise ourselves.

I sit just inside the doorway of the tent, working with releasing all fear, breathing slowly in, slowly out. *No fear here. There is no fear here.* I tell myself and try to project an aura of protection around us. I talk in silence to Bear.

This is our space, and we will fight to protect it. No fear here. There is no fear here. This is our space, and we will fight to protect it. I'll gouge your eyes, and I'll stick my hand so far down your throat... I'll fight if I have to, but we mean you no harm.

Now she is at the door of the tent. She stops sniffing. Silence fills the world like the empty moment after a loon's rising call falls back into the lake. She pushes her head through the open-door flaps and into the tent, gently stretching its fabric. Her two eyes look into mine. My eyes look into hers. *We are not afraid. I will fight to protect.*

Breathe, Larry. Be relaxed and ready. Breathe!

An ancient, even primal, knowledge awakens. *I know you from all the history of mankind and bears!* This knowing is felt as a kind of waking up within the very cellular structure of my body. It expands to fill me like the concentric rings of a pebble landing in a pond.

I have hunted and been hunted. I have worshiped, eaten, and been eaten. We have even shared the same cave out of desperation to be sure, uncomfortable as it was. We are old neighbors, old family.

I look into the eyes of an old god, a scavenger, an omnivore, and a predator.

I inhale her exhalation, and she, in turn, inhales mine. We breathe in synchrony the very same air, each in turn, as if we are one being, and I am a bear.

I am Bear.

I am just out wandering through the woods like I always do, following my nose and curiosity, looking for something to eat, for something to satisfy my belly. Now...

This *Now* is an eternity for me. I cannot say how long this forever is, though it surely is only seconds. It is long enough, however, to change my life, for me to die, and to be reborn.

My return to this world is like the gentle teasing apart from one consciousness into two, as though a single ball of cotton is being gently separated from itself. Once again, I look into the eyes of a bear, but now with a new awareness, an observer's perspective of what I am doing. There is an ironic sense of simply wishing her a nice day and then—

She withdraws her head from the tent and walks off into the early morning shadows of the forest, disappears into the tall and ancient pines, only to live a life of her own within me.

This is a time of madness in my life. My divorce from Lisa is finalized that summer. Aunt Eudene's suicide visits me some nights, like an invitation into the release and comfort of a long sleep. I am my grandfather's child. I drink, smoke hash and pot, and forget my shame of being alive, of not being the son my parents want me to be, of not possessing the faith God requires for the grace of his salvation.

I am in open rebellion against the world, against God, against a criminal government at war in Vietnam, and a President of the United States who lied to me, to us. I take it personally.

So it is that Bear saves my life. Many times, and again, she does. Which is why I think of myself as being *born of Bear*.

Many a night I think of killing myself. I consider how: gun, rope, car or... And then I remember: Bear! Her simple presence. Her lush beauty. Traveling into the depths of her liquid eyes. The wildness. Her breath.

I remember touching... consciousness, her... presence, until there was only one of us. I remember the wondrous mystery of becoming Bear, of accessing a deep resource of knowledge spanning time, space, species, identity, and self. *Maybe there is something special about me after all*, I think. *Maybe I'm being initiated like Carlos Castaneda with Don Juan. Maybe I am Christ... This experience of wonder and mystery is worth living into...*

And I choose to live through one more night.

And then, for one more day, I live too.

Sarah and I break up soon after our return to Detroit. I work eighty-hour weeks and drink-and-drug myself to sleep at night, alone, or with a woman whenever possible. God, if my parents knew, if they suspected my intimacy with these hungers, such longings of heart and body, they would personally lead me by the hand to the Gates of Hell.

Their voice has, in fact, become my voice. *"What is it with you, Larry? You're nothing but an animal. Christ said, 'But I say to you that whoever looks at a woman to lust for her has already committed adultery with her in his heart' (Matthew 5:28). Don't you have any respect for God, for his Holy Word?"*

"Do you want to spend eternity in Hell? Burning in flames? That's where you're headed, son. You know the scripture. We raised you to respect it. To love God. You're a worthless wretch. Your life is not worth living—without God."

"You better repent, turn again from your evil ways. Ask God for forgiveness. You know what he did to Sodom and Gomorrah. You're nothing but a worthless sinner. You're the worst kind too—you know better. You'd be better to never have been born."

"You're an alcoholic too. Drinking all the time. We taught you better. You are a drug addict, smoking all that pot and taking all those other things. We don't even know what they are. But we know they come from the Devil. They are Evil. Just like you. You are going to die alone in some dirty gutter."

"Just look at yourself. Smoking cigarettes, of all things. Nasty. Dirty. Smelly stuff. You're addicted to it. You know your body is the temple of God. Why don't you treat it as such?"

"And you hang out in bars! We told you those places would get you in trouble. No good ever walked out of one of them. You hang out with the wrong kind of friends. You have not been to church in years. You have forsaken the Lord God. You don't even pray to him anymore. We're ashamed of you. What kind of example are you for God? Don't you know everybody is watching you? Judging us, your dad, as a preacher, by your behavior?"

Their judgments sleep with me as companions. Their condemnations chase me through my dreams and haunt me like anonymous whispers leaking out of every group of people I walk through.

It is during this time that the journal keeping, out of desperation, begins to prove its life-saving value for me. For it helps me to reflect and realize that it is my very hatred of Dad, and of God, that gives them such power in my life. *The more I hate Dad, the more like him I become,* I write in my journal.

The more I study and struggle with this issue of how humans embody, like unseen shadows, the characteristics they despise and detest in others, the more uncomfortable I become with myself. The worst is a growing awareness of similarities between Dad and me; how much like the man I hate I am.

Dad finds his meaning for life in work. So do I.

Dad finds his meaning for life in something outside himself. Me too.

Dad doesn't know how to talk about anything but his work. Neither do I.

Dad doesn't know how to relate to people apart from his work. I don't either. We both use work as our primary means of identity. I'm a workaholic. Addicted to staying busy, to a politics of my social equality and justice, to helping people.

Dad doesn't know how to relax, relate, and just be with people for the enjoyment of it. Neither do I.

In fact, Dad doesn't know how to play. Neither do I, except with the aid of drugs.

Dad doesn't know how to laugh. Neither do I, except with the aid of drugs.

Dad is married to a woman who mothers him, bolsters his ego, and makes up for his personal deficiencies of social inadequacy. Got me again.

Dad uses work to, I suspect, avoid looking at the pain of his own life—his own childhood. I work till exhaustion makes it difficult to stand, and then I take drugs to give my body sensations besides emotional pain to focus on.

I suspect Dad of feeling innately inadequate for life. I often think of killing myself. In fact, I suspect the Glover clan of carrying a depressive, if not self-destructive, or suicidal gene. His father and sister died of suicide—my granddad and aunt. One of Dad's brothers, my uncle, cut off one of his testicles, and then apparently spent time in a mental hospital. What was that self-mutilation all about? How much fear of God and shame of body did that take?

Another Glover uncle was killed, accidentally, in a hunting accident. Another Glover uncle died when he and his friends gassed up their car and tried to drive off without paying—got shot by the station attendant. A son of one of his brothers, my cousin, was killed by a pistol in an argument with another driver. Other cousins struggle with schizophrenia and depression...

Dad seems to find his only sense of worth in life in saving souls. I find my only sense of worth and value when I'm helping someone. However, my personal boundaries are so diffuse that I'm unable to separate the pain and suffering of clients from my own. They come home with me at night and sleep with me in my nightmares.

Dad and I both can be cruel and mean, can enjoy inflicting pain, and are both highly self-righteous and judgmental of others. And yet we both find pleasure in helping people!

I am so like the man I've tried so hard not to be like!

Becoming Man

Until a man has hung
suspended by the North Star
naked and upside down
then buried and eaten by worms
and been born again
into milkweed and monarch
into wild rose and honeybee
unto a woman squatting naked on soil of African Earth
with legs spread in prayer
under the darkness of a full moon—
with their shared placenta offered
back into the earth of their nourishment

he is not yet a man
but only a pretense of one
trying to be
whom he believes
he should be

But if hanging
upon this cross of his humanity
proves his heart courageous enough to surrender
and the eye of his mind willing to see
world and self—anew
he discovers a grace within
and himself blessed

with a knowledge of belonging
as a wild joy rises
quenching spirit and soul of thirst
as a gift only received by those
drinking directly from spring's source

Chapter 7

BORN ANEW—OF WATER AND OF SPIRIT

I moved in with Jennifer within a couple of months of our first meeting. She has a couple of young sons and lives in an old farmhouse outside a Northern Michigan tourist town. I come home a day early from a trip, expecting a delightful and sensuous reunion. A pickup in the driveway alerts me to expect one of her old friends perhaps having coffee at the kitchen table. But no.

Jennifer stumbles down the stairs as she pulls a long-sleeved white shirt onto her sexy naked body. It was the same shirt she wore when we first met, with her two erect nipples competing for attention with her two unwavering blue eyes. All hope I have for the making of a new life runs out the door as rage and fury storm in.

Like swallowing tears unshed, my domesticated masculine powers of running from hard feelings, at twenty-six years old, are now a habituated pattern and I'm ready to get out of town faster than possible. Physical possessions are stripped to what fits in the back of my truck and may be necessary for living a life on the road. Mother's assertion that "life is not worth living without God" haunts my nights and days.

I stop by the folk's place for a last visit, to say my goodbyes, and to let them know I don't know when or if I'll ever see 'em again.

Tension fills the room and conversation as we three sit around a four-chair dining table. Dad, almost in confession to the empty chair, says, "The reason I whipped you so much was because I thought you had too much pride."

He follows me out the door to my truck as I leave. "We used to be proud of you," he says, looking at me as the two of us stand beside the door of the truck. I turn away to open the door as he, too, turns to walk away.

I climb into the cab of Ole Blue, my seventeen-year-old beloved Chevy pickup, slam the door, and barely survive the drive to a friend's home, back in Detroit's inner city. A semitruck rides the edge of my freeway lane with tires screaming, pushing me close to a concrete abutment on the driver's side.

A quick turn of the wheel and it'll all be over for me. That'd make the folks sorry. And no one would ever know...and the damn truck is about to push me there anyway and... How easy this could be...

It is the narrowest of escapes.

I stay with friends for a few days of numbing together, do a final pack on Ole Blue for the road, throw a heavy green canvas tarp over the back, and head west on I-94 out of Detroit. There is no geographic destination in mind. I am in search of Self.

I remember traveling through Idaho a year back, when David, Skip, and I took the Drive-a-way car to Vancouver, WA. That was a fun trip, and I'd like to go back there.

God, the country was incredible! Lots of wilderness land there. That's starting to feel like a compass needle pointing to magnetic north. I need to get away from people. Away from every expectation of personal identity, my own or anybody else's.

I feel like I've been taking a whirlwind of gut-wrenching blows, for years, in love, family, and religion. And I am dazed and disoriented in a social jungle where only need or willful delusion allows me to believe in the integrity of government by the people, for the people. I am angry. In a rage. Hurting. Lost.

Seeking out wild country, for a resolution to my life's confusion, is an awakening instinct. *If I find a wild place into which I can disappear, never to be heard from again, that feels inviting. Anything to just stop all this pain. Death doesn't sound so bad. I would like to control the time of her arrival, though.*

Fear and adrenaline entwine, without distinction, as I shoulder my backpack with a heavy seven days' worth of food. *Took a six-pack of beer and a joint to get me packed up. I've never spent more than two days out alone before. I feel so alone in the world that this physical solitude feels confirming of reality.*

Walking away from my truck, I anticipate the possibility that I might never come out. The thought of someplace without all this hurt, where I might simply stop existing, someplace alone, never to be found or judged, draws me down the trail like a magnet.

I'm gonna come back a different man—or I'm not coming back at all. Life is just too frigging painful. It's not worth the struggle and suffering.

I'm resiliently stuck in a life not worth living. I'm even condemned and haunted by a God I don't even believe in anymore!

God, parents, religion, government... I can't even separate you from each other. You're all evil! There's no way to really escape somehow being part of destroying the earth. How does one stand against this hypocritical God's Country, waging war in Nam, killing innocent women and children?

I've seen how my own efforts to do good result in a runaway kid returning to an abusive home too many times to count.

And damn it, *Jennifer! God, I'd just moved in with you and was ready to really give it a go, and then I come home and you're in bed with some guy. Damn! That really hurt, Jennifer. We'd just had days and nights of incredible sex. Now, I can't stop pulling up and seeing the strange truck in the drive, walking into the house and then you rushing down the stairs with hair a mess and wearing only that white cotton half-buttoned shirt.*

Such memories and thoughts haunt me as I march through seven miles of snow-drifted trail into the remote Middle Fork of the Salmon River country. It's early spring yet, and I'm desperate enough to break a knee-deep trail through many a virgin drift. The trail winds its way to the river's edge along the canyon bottom, and I'm thinking I'll just follow the water and my instincts as far away from my life as possible.

The roar of the river's raging current almost pushes me from behind, along the right side of the river. The rugged trail comes to the face of a small cliff. I cannot believe what lies in front of me.

No! My heart screams. *Not this! I can't go back. But what am I gonna do? I Am Not Going Back!*

The rocky trail ahead just drops straight down into a little dip, a drainage crossing, and it's filled with water, boiling and tumbling and rumbling up against the cliff face. And the trail... the trail just disappears!

Looks like it gets deep too. Too deep to even think of trying to walk through it. And damn, that water's moving fast! All this spring runoff crashing up against the rock. Options. Options. There's gotta be some other options!

I look to the ridge rising above, thinking maybe to climb up and around this solid and liquid swirl of chaos. *That's a damn steep and rugged mix of scree and cliff face. There's no stability anywhere. High as I can see. It's a sure death sentence.*

Look again at what's in front of you, Larry. Movement in the river alongside me catches my eye. It's a giant uprooted ponderosa pine tree! It races downriver past me, amid splashing, translucent, greenish, white-capped waves and large blocks of snow and ice. *Damn!*

Look close, Larry. This is absolute insanity if you decide to climb this! I study the textures and structures of the face and see only the smallest of nubbins.

I ain't going back. I don't care what. I ain't going back now.

I study harder. Plan. Okay, there's one possible hold for my left hand, then my left foot can stretch out, carefully, out above the turbulence for… yeah! That little nub. Then, that's the point of commitment— putting weight onto those holds for the transfer of the right hand to… Yeah, there may be. Oh yeah. And then the right foot to there.

Then there's that little one and, yeah, that'd make three moves out. And that's about a fourth of the way across, so…

I'm going for it. Damn! There's another uprooted tree floating downstream! I'm gonna unbuckle my waist belt. If I do fall in, the first thing I want to do is shed this pack. I don't want to be like a fish on land; floundering around in the freezing river, trying to catch my breath while fighting to get rid of my pack. No. I'll dump the pack quickly, then be ready to die in peace, without fighting the river!

My heart drums in my chest and ears. I commit.

Once I've made the three moves out onto the face that I'd planned on, I find I can gain a little extra left-arm-reach by turning my head to the right, away from my intended direction of travel. *There! Got it!*

But it's not very good. Damn it! I'm gonna look for something else and I go to turn my head back to the left slowly, to see what I might reach for. But I am pressed vertically into the cliff, with the top of my pack wedged against the back of my head. An instantaneous warning shiver flashes throughout every cell in my body as I just start the turn.

That ain't gonna work! Okay. Calm down, Larry.

With my head still facing toward the trail on my right, I determine to try again finding a hold on the left. *Maybe there's something more secure.* My left hand sweeps blindly across the rock for irregularities of promise. *Nothing!*

Damn! My legs quiver lightly from the strain of the heavy pack and the slight rock edges the rims of my boot soles rest on. Fingertips threaten to slip off their dubious holds. My immediate craving is to get the hell off the rock and back onto solid ground. As quick as a wish would not be too soon.

I find, however, that I cannot undo my last move—the move that would allow me to reach back toward the still nearby solidity of the trail. *I need the advantage of that little extra-arm-reach gained when I turned my head to the right.* A very careful repeated attempt to turn my head to the left, so that I can make the reach of return to my right, sends an electric shock through my body—the feeling of, *I just almost fell!*

I fight against the panic struggling to overtake my entire being. The debilitating panic that would have me give up in the face of irrational odds. With my fingers feeling like they might slip at any time, and the vibration of my leg muscles threatening to spasm right off their tenuous placements, I fight the panic that wants to wash over me like a tsunami.

I fight against the hysteria that says, *Give up, Larry. You don't stand a chance. You're going to fall—drown in a freezing river—your body never found.*

This is an instinctive struggle for my last moments of life. But there, there on the cliff, in my fight for whatever mental, emotional, and physical control of my life I can find, I remember Bear.

Bear, emptying her lungs before sniffing air in again. And I begin to breathe with more intention and awareness than ever before. One slow inhalation, followed by a slow exhalation. Like a hungry person savoring what they expect to be their life's last few tastes of food, I relished the in-breaths, breathing in until I sense that another molecule of air in my lungs might just be enough to push me off the cliff. I revel in the exhalations too—discover the more I breathe out, the more I can let go of—the more I can allow in.

And so, my body and mind focus intensely on breathing out every molecule of air... out, out, out... I push the air out from my belly into the emptiness of no breath. I savor this pause into stillness...

Then slowly my body begins the conscious inhale of air molecules, seemingly one at a time to start. Then, as my belly and chest fill to where they ever so gently embrace subtle contours on the rock face, the pause into stillness arrives again, before the slow release of air begins again.

Yet because I feel most physically secure on the cliff when I am empty of air, I place more and more emphasis upon my exhalations, but always taking note of the last molecules, whether out or in. I discover an exquisite sensuality in simply breathing in as deeply and out as exhaustively as possible. I notice, with my attention focused so intently on breathing, that my sense of panic is releasing its grip on me. And there is a growing sense of mental, emotional, and physical control. And so, I sink into the experience even more, until eventually, I notice—*I am being breathed. The body knows how! All on its own!*

Death still feels imminent, but I begin to sense that within the power of conscious attention lies the power to transform my living. *I may well die here, but I can choose to control how I shall meet this dying.*

You can be full of fear, fighting and flailing your arms and legs upon hitting the ice-cold white-water lapping near your boots, Larry, sucking desperately for air. Or you can find a way to meet death with a dignity of acceptance you've never felt in life before.

Pinned against that cliff face like an insect, I begin to sense a personal dignity, a sense of control and power lying within attention to my breath. *On some elemental level, their origin, and presence are already inside me, awaiting some kind of intention or focus to wake up.*

All my senses continue with a kind of opening attunement. The sound of white water around me is a playful chorus of sweet music and voices singing. The colors of the yellow and orange lichen on the rock take on a radiant brilliance. I take note of the sun's angle behind me, as cloud flows alternately throw shadows or reveals sunlight. The molecules in my fingertips and boot soles began to meld into the rock I cling to.

And I decide, live or die, I will breathe my last breath consciously, without fear. *My real challenge is to walk into either experience breathing, maximizing attention and control. I give myself to the embrace of whatever might come, with all the awareness I can muster.*

I complete all but the last three moves across the cliff face blind, moving to my left. Trusting my breath, some inner bodily intuition and intelligence and eros that are not even on my inherited map of reality.

Upon stepping onto the trail's firm footing I have been dreaming of, my body hungrily sucks in a deep and full breath, which then explodes with a literal scream of discovery. "I'm alive!"

It feels so delicious to be so awake. I scream it out into the world again. But this time with intention, as if I were still on the cliff. I consciously attend to the slow exhalation and surrender into emptiness, pause there and witness, then savor the body's impulse for breathing in. I consciously suck in all the air I can and then savor the depth of meaning in each word as I scream each syllable: "I—am—a-live!"

I buckle the waistbelt and cinch up my pack before hiking again. My body comes to an abrupt stop in about fifteen feet. I am dumbfounded and unbelieving of what lies at my feet in the middle of the trail. *It is the skin of a snake, left in its shedding.*

Life becomes a dream as I continue deeper into the wilds within and without, all an unfolding of the mystery of existence, one beyond descriptions of words and naming. It's all too enormous for such delusional boxes of containment.

I sleep under and nestle among the roots of ancient elder pine trees, in beds shared with deer, elk, and mountain lion. Eagle circles overhead. And I breathe in, as companions, the smells of forest and river, soil and stars. And Bear. The eyes and breath and the lumbering easy belonging walk and presence of Bear is never far from me.

My body and spirit continue to breathe in and revel in the ecstatic eroticism of a new embodiment: *I am alive!*

I overflow with gratitude, with a wild joy of celebration for this simple awareness. What a gift! What a marvel! What a wonder this is…to be alive! So too, related sentiments reflecting new depths of somatic realizations become like mantras through my days and dreams.

This life… this life is mine to live. I alone own this life. I alone am responsible for what I do with it… how I meet it. There is no more blaming God or Dad or others.

So long as I live in this breath… this breath alone… this inhalation… this exhalation… the story of identity I live and tell is mine to create.

What Freedom! What Responsibility! To live this life as Mystery, as an enormous womb of unfolding creation, consciously choosing the placement of my attention.

I return to Ole Blue days later, a new man, born anew. Of this, I am sure. The integrations of these *altered state experiences* spiral yet decades ahead into the future and continue still.

I'm pushing the engine on Old Blue into third gear up a long, steep, and narrow mountain pass when around a curve in the road, blazing downhill toward me, is a large sparkling red pickup truck hauling a shiny aluminum Airstream trailer. Smoke billows out a vent on the roof, and my body screams, "Fire!" In a flash, in my rearview mirror, they are gone out of sight around a curve behind me just as fast as they first appeared.

They're completely unaware they are fanning the flames of demise with their speed. Just like humanity, driving climate change denial into a future of self-destruction, I think.

Days later, I'm enjoying the festive spirits and women in short shorts and halter tops at a craft fair in Eugene, OR. I'm on my way to a little Northern California town, hoping to get laid. *Was a sweet night, the one we had, when we met so... maybe... just maybe?*

I'm trying not to stare impolitely, aware of the masculine predator energy of religious and cultural inheritance. And I am soaking in the alluring femininity of two embodied divine goddesses, as I am yet learning to view women. Their conversation is animated and overflowing with depths of wisdom. Like this transformational observation, one says to the other, "If people just knew how to breathe... there wouldn't be any more political oppression or wars."

The phrase lands in my heart and haunts me through the coming years. *If people just knew how to breathe… there wouldn't be any more political oppression or wars.*

Breathing is culturally forbidden! Why? Damn interesting inquiry!

The next evening, continuing my trip down to California, I decide it is better to drive late into the night's wee hours than make camp in a drizzling rain.

The early morning light has that two-a.m.-darkness to it as I drive the back road, a quiet and near-deserted narrow two-lane-highway, from Portland down to Eugene. A light, steady Oregon drizzle cools the night air. Jackson Browne sings *Rosie* on the tape player.

For company, I relive and create conversations with all the women in my life—the ones I left, and the ones who left me. *One thing was for sure, I sure wasn't raised to expect how a lot of women like sex as much as I do! Hell, I come from the religious tradition of putting pants on piano legs, so as to not tempt the men!*

I thought it was just supposed to be men who are doing the hunting, but… damn! Women can sure be hungry for it too, and some of 'em can have a lot of orgasms and just go on and on, forever! I get horny just remembering and thinking about this woman down in CA. We sure had a fun night together! Lisa and I just used to do it under the covers, but… I still hurt from leaving her. I really screwed her over. And I still love her! I'm all fucked up!

The unfamiliar, winding two-lane road and rainy conditions remind me to keep my altered attention on driving. A Boone's Farm bottle of wine is stashed between my legs for convenience, however, and a hash pipe is in my left hand. The lighter is in my right, just as I round a corner.

Headlights flash through the fog onto a lone hitchhiker standing on the side of the road. *He is so out of place on this black rainy night. Damn, I passed him even as I saw him. The rain and darkness sure hid him. Almost made him look fuzzy.*

Maybe it's a holdover from my liking Jesus's story of the good Samaritan as a kid. I often pick up hitchhikers or pull over to help folks with flat tires or other needs. But there's something here that calls for alertness. *He's got to be cold, standing out in this drizzle, this time of night, middle of nowhere, and in a T-shirt. Guess I'll pick him up, but be careful, Larry. This guy might be crazy.* I take note of and laugh at how I talk out loud to myself all the time. It comes from spending a lot of time alone.

I pull over, begin backing up a bit, and then, in the rearview mirror, see him running toward me. I stop and let him close the distance while I scramble to stash the bottle and smoke. The hitchhiker opens the passenger door, just as I'm making room for him on the truck's bench seat, quickly throwing various things to new places. The dome light comes on as the door opens and my Buck hunting knife is in my right hand.

I thought I'd throw it onto the passenger side dash, but catch myself mid-throw, freeze, and question the wisdom of this placement. All this, too, just as the hitchhiker and I have the opportunity for our first lighted and brief check of each other. Then we both take note of the knife in my hand. I decide to continue the throw of the knife as an indication of trust and confidence.

He climbs on in and shuts the door quickly, as if to keep out something else that might want in. The dome light goes out with the sound of the slamming door. The quiet is suddenly loud. We each wait alone for our eyes to readjust to the natural darkness of the night.

Finally, I stick out my hand. "I'm Larry."

Silence again fills the truck. No one moves. *Maybe he can't see my hand in the dark*, I think. I withdraw my hand.

I figure it is my truck and the next move is mine. So, I return his silence and allow it to sit between us. My hungry eyes search for his in the truck's dark cab. When our eyes finally meet, my passenger speaks.

"I'm going to kill you," he says. His eyes now seem to burn with an inner flame as he stares into mine.

Immediately, however, I feel Bear within me as a protector. I also find myself back on the cliff face. Spontaneously and consciously, I slow and deepen my breath until I am again breathing what feels to be molecules of air, one at a time. We each stare into the eyes of the other. Time loses all linearity and goes nowhere. There is only *this* moment. My consciousness sinks into my belly. With my breathing slowed, I feel centered. Wholly present. Without fear. And I see into my would-be assassin.

Funny, I think, *he looks like me. Except his ears are almost pointed. And the way his hair comes down matted and pointed like that in the front. God! He looks just like Satan! The Devil!*

The surrealism of the situation startles me. A dream-like quality holds the two of us together, like two climbers sharing destiny because of a rope between them. I fight to breathe deliberately. Doing so returns to me a sense of control, of calm.

My bloodstream runs with adrenaline. I do not doubt his stated intention. Only a few feet separate our faces. I know death sits across from me. The acuity of my physical and intuitive senses heightens. I sniff...

He smells of fear and of anger. Most of all, he is lonely and very confused. Scared. But how dangerous is he?

He's clearly desperate, being out here in the middle of nowhere on this cool, dark, rainy night. And with only a T-shirt and pants.

I instinctively know I dare not break eye contact, or cease to count molecules, for in this space, I possess the confidence of self-control. I am ready for whatever might come. If it is to be death, I will enter with my eyes open, looking to see what I might find.

I catch myself foolishly noting and reveling in the recently discovered powers of my consciousness, for maintaining composure and self-control, and shift focus back onto my would-be passenger. He is me! I am him! I suddenly know neither quite who is who. It is as though I tranced into him and am on the edge of getting lost but now need to distill apart and remember who is who.

Breathe Larry! Slowly! Deliberately! Explore the whole space of your lungs, their emptiness, their fullness!

This mindful breathing returns me to myself. The next move still belongs to me. Our gaze remains unbroken. I sense my partner becoming uncomfortable with my lack of response. This tells me the time for taking control is now.

"Listen, friend!" I speak each syllable deliberately, slowly. Even the spaces of silence between words have meaning as I continue. Each word is an island in a song of meaning.

"This is my truck. If you need a ride, I'll give you one. But if you are thinking about giving me any trouble, you can get out right now."

A thick silence returns to the cab of the truck. It lasts nearly an eternity before I break it. "So, what's it going to be?" Our eye-to-eye connection remains unbroken.

My passenger continues staring at me with hatred. Then he glances but briefly down toward the floor of the truck, as if involuntarily revealing an unwanted insecurity. He immediately re-established the challenge coming from his stare into my eyes. After this last ineffectual attempt at dominance, however, he looks to the floor again. He leaves his gaze there. I have the sense he would now roll over onto his back like a submissive dog, revealing his neck and belly, if I command.

I give Jerry a ride.

In the last dark before dawn, I pull into a pull-off rest area for a short sleep, so as not to arrive in town too early. I give Jerry a wool blanket and the bed of the truck, where I usually sleep. I stretch out uncomfortably in the cab with my sleeping bag over me. I lock the doors; crack the windows slightly open for air and hope the mosquitos will not find their way in.

I wake to Jerry screaming and my body involuntarily bolting upright. Maybe thirty yards away, Jerry stands below the driver's cab door of a parked semi-truck. His fists are raised in the air. He shakes them in challenge to the invisible occupant and proceeds to scream obscenities about the driver's mother.

"Shit!" I scramble out of my bag and the truck and run over to try to quiet the man down. I fear for both our safety, should an angry and tire-iron welding truck driver appear.

I get Jerry back into the bed of Old Blue. I was now too restless and afraid to sleep, however. We drive to a twenty-four-hour truck stop. We both order two eggs over easy, hash browns, bacon, toast, and coffee. As he had on the drive down during the night, Jerry again mumbled something to me like, "I know who you are. You're the guy who turned me in. You got me locked up. You turned me in, man. Want me to suck your dick?"

"No. And if you don't shut up and stop staring at the waitress like that, I am going to take your food and coffee away," I threaten in return. Jerry hungrily shovels his breakfast down but interrupts the flow to twist his whole body to stare obviously at the waitress's cute butt whenever she walks by. People in nearby booths are starting to stare at us.

When we are both done eating, I am fully awash in the emotions of again not knowing what helping is. *What do I do with this guy? Give him to the police? Who knows what they'll do to him? They sure won't help him, anyway. He's just a hippy vagabond to them, and not even a local one! I hate to turn him loose on the world, but maybe I just have to trust the universe to do what it needs, or what it will.*

Breathing consciously all the while, to keep my emotions controlled, I give Jerry the wool blanket, an old coat I liked, and some money. Then I put him out at an intersection of his choosing.

I do not know how to pray. Or who to pray to, but I do my best. I ask the Great Spirit of the universe to take care of Jerry, and of whoever he might next encounter.

Looking in the rear-view mirror as I drive off, Jerry looks dazed, confused, and lost. Standing there in my old green army coat, with the wool blanket rolled up and hung over his back with a short rope, the light drizzle starting again, he looks like someone the police will probably pick up shortly.

Help him, Great Spirit, I pray. I don't know how.

I find a liquor store just opening, then I drive out into the hills and find a lake and a place I can camp. I get stumbling drunk and stoned, way into the night, and by the crackling sounds and light of a campfire.

I don't know what to do with all the pain. There is just too much pain in the world. Too many people are hurting. God, I hurt! I just don't know how to live with all this pain.

What If I Were to Tell You

Everything you learned in church and school
of who you are
is wrong?

You know the uncomfortable truth of this.

But how will you live
with this shattering awareness?

How will you navigate and find your way,
you blind one walking tales of creation
by candlelight, amidst galaxies milky with stars
above, below, and within?

Sometimes it might feel easier to just forget
you ever glimpsed such wondrous light.
Tempting, not to open the invitation
into this radical ownership of your life.

But then you remember and sense, like a seed awakening,
the aliveness and joy of living
into a Mystery older than words
as it blossoms into
an identity of innate belonging and worthiness.

Wild Joy

And so it is you recall
what it is to rest in the womb of the Great Mother,
what it is to suckle at the spring's source—
the thirst-quenching Waters of Life,

every sip in-forming the truth of who you are.

Chapter 8

RESURRECTION OF THE SACRED—
THE ECOLOGICAL SELF

Selling my blood for gas money and spending my last quarter on a cup of coffee, before dumpster-diving behind a grocery store for food, makes for a long winter in Northern Idaho. I'm excited to receive an early-season temporary position with the Payette National Forest, out of McCall, come spring. I feel my chest swell from just the thought of being a forest firefighter.

Our early-season days are spent driving the forest, with me getting to know the country and the more seasoned men I work with. We cut fallen trees to open roads, clear trails, put up Smokey signs, paint buildings, check stock fences, and clean and pick up trash around guard stations and campgrounds. I spend a lot of time in the cabin of a pickup truck with one or two other men, depending on the day, driving to distant job sites. Lunch pails and steel thermoses of impatient steaming coffee accompany us.

There are three of us when I go out on my first big-tree fire. I am with John and Jack. John is the senior crew member, of local early immigrant Basque heritage, and proud of it. He can be moody, but also likes to laugh as much as spit Red Man snuff. He wears a handlebar mustache that is as long as his face is narrow. When I first see him pull his white Stetson cowboy hat off, I'm surprised to see the shiny bald head under it.

Jack is an athletic younger man with an abundance of cynical humor that starts many of my days with a smile. A helicopter drops the three of us off in a mountain meadow, as close to a fire as I will ever again be laid down. It is a whopping big spruce tree sitting alone in the middle of the grassy field, hit by lightning, with flames dramatically roaring out the top. A hole in the trunk, several feet down from the apparently rotten top, creates a wood-chimney.

Some part of me hurts with the thought of falling and taking the life of this magnificent old tree, but who am I to question Smokey, and his saying we got to take it down? We get to work, saving the forest.

The challenge immediately facing us, however, is that the length of our chainsaw's blade is roughly half the diameter of the tree, making the falling process all the more dangerous. Our radio call for a larger saw is denied. All the bigger saws are out on other fires. So we begin to beaver our way through this massive, nearly eighty-foot-tall tree of about five-foot diameter. Fire falls out of the top of the tree. Burning coals roll out the bottom of the chimney and drop onto the sawyer. Branches and debris fall. The danger of the top burning through and falling is real.

I am alive! I've finally gotten a job where I can do no harm, and it's an exciting job to boot—fighting evil forest fires, adrenalin-filled helicopter flights, and getting the bonus of hazard pay increases the sense of adventure. Seeing the size of this big tree we are going to cut, I sense I am an initiate in an ancient ritual into a certain kind of manhood.

There is also a clear sense of ceremony to the awareness of safety as we set up a rotating system of cutting on the tree. We post a lookout at a distance enough to see the top and ready to holler when any fire or debris falls from the tree, and a spotter stands close, ready to tap the shoulder of the sawyer if he needs to move out of the way fast. Given that I'm the neophyte on such fires, I'm given the honor of making the final cut on this magnificent tree. I start making the backcut, the final cut in the tree-felling process. It is made on the opposite side and above the initial two cuts, designed to leave a pie or wedge-shaped opening where one wants the tree to fall. I watch the width of the saw-blade's cut closely, strategically removing the remaining wood holding the tree upright. Even a micro-narrowing of the backcut's width might disastrously pinch the saw's blade, not only pinching or locking the saw in place, but perhaps lead to the tree falling opposite to its intended direction.

The slightest enlargement of the backcut's width foretells the beginning of the tree's fall in the intended direction. I note the slightest opening of the backcut's width just as John, standing right behind me as safety, taps my shoulder to make sure I know gravity now owns this tree's fall. I turn the saw off and move to safety.

The tree crashes to Earth with a thunder that makes the ground shake under my feet. A deafening silence announces itself, as if the whole forest acknowledges with honor the fall of this ancient one, even as the treetop explodes upon impact. It is as if a bomb went off, as flaming hot coals and fire are thrown throughout the brushy area it lands in.

John and Jack come up to me with congratulatory handshakes and backslaps. And Jack says, "Don't that just make your dick hard?"

It doesn't. But I do feel the allurements of adrenaline and testosterone, and the accompanying feelings of power, control, and domination. I also feel like I'm one of the guys. Like I belong, though there is a haunting sense of shadowy entanglements among these various feelings.

I still feel like a preacher's kid in hiding, running from my own history, socially insecure, and trying to break free of some nebulous sense of captivity.

Given these insecurities, it doesn't take long to realize I need some things for my manly uniform if I'm going to fit in. Uniforms are like that. I need a cowboy hat. A knife to wear on my belt. Pants cut short so as not to get caught in the brush. And a pair of those logger's boots, without the steel toes, of course—high-heeled, thick-soled, and deep-treaded, tall, black leather boots. Custom-made Whites out of Seattle are the best, and worth the expense. *I already have the drinking part down. But I also need to chew tobacco, to complete my uniform and be one of the guys*, I think.

When I put that first wad of sweet, damp, bitter Red Man chew in my mouth, my stomach wants to come right up my throat. I hold it down though, swallow it like a man. Before too long, I am sucking and spitting tobacco like I'd nursed on it.

Later, I work with Dick, a young man fresh out of the Marines who still sports his military haircut. When we run in the evenings, for the hour of fitness training we're allowed, Dick runs in his boots. I train in my running shoes. It's a stretch for me to keep pace with him.

We are cutting grass in a field around a guard station for fire protection. The grass is over a foot tall, and the gasoline mower will not do the job. We take turns with the scythe, a tool with an ancient history, a long curved wooden handle, and a long knife-sharp curved blade. It is nearly a hundred degrees out, and the sun beats down on us.

"Pussy snuff," he calls my Skoal brand, which is already a step up from the weaker Red Man. "Why don't you try some real tobacco?" he challenges, then spits and offers me a pinch of his Copenhagen.

It is my turn on the scythe when Dick reaches out with his can of tobacco. How could I not meet his challenge? Salty sweat drips off me from exertion and the sun's intense heat. We both work with our shirts off. I am still learning the rhythm and use of the tool, and how to let the swing move through my whole body. The sun sits on my head. I feel lightheaded from the tobacco. And then I feel sick. My stomach wants to wretch, but I cannot allow that.

I hold it. Vile bile spurts up into the back of my throat in a teasing threat. I swallow the bitterness back down. Finally, it is Dick's turn on the scythe again. He kindly makes no comment about my green color. I hand over the scythe, turn my back to him as I walk away, and use a finger to sweep the Cope out of my mouth, from between cheek and gum.

But a month later, I've switched to 'the real man's tobacco.' It is a stronger high. Soon too, I learned not to spit—just swallow the juice instead. Spitting is too inconvenient. Especially in grocery stores or restaurants, and even in a bar. Besides, after first learning to wash the juice down with beer, learning to swallow it straight comes easy. Shortly, tobacco is a constant companion. It is the first thing I put in my mouth in the morning. The last thing I take out at night. I learn to eat with it corralled between the cheek and gum. I drink beer and lean against the bar in Lardos Saloon, swallow my chew juice, lust after the pretty women, and feel a strident self-sufficiency, despite my loneliness. I just take another dip and swallow more of those familiar juices.

It is the perfect addiction for me, not nearly as inconvenient as smoking. Or as obvious. I can run a chainsaw or dig fire lines and chew. Many of the men do it. And with the strength of Cope, I could have a small pinch of chew if need be and people don't even know I'm sucking on it—that I am sucking on vile juices. On poison. Shame and pain.

It is the perfect addiction for me. Fits right in with learning to swallow my voice, needs, and desires as a kid, and my emotions as a man. Now, while trying to rediscover their legitimacy, I simultaneously confirm my old fears of a secret flaw, and announce my masculine strength and self-sufficiency, all with the convenience of a chew. I have not found anything as useful as an addiction for simultaneously crawling away from my feelings while also bringing the sense of a mother's comfort.

But I'm a man now. Hell, I've been initiated!

And I'm getting paid to live and work in nature. In the wilds! And I'll get winters off 'cause there ain't no other jobs to be had round here, what with the lumber mill's closing. I can write, read, cross-country ski, hit the hot springs, and soak with naked women...

"Get the guys together," our foreman, Dave, tells me one day. "We're going down to the South Fork and do some work at the guard station there."

I come to understand the station itself has been unmanned for years. Efforts are made to keep it usable, however, in case of need.

Six of us climb into the two pickups. It is a fourteen-mile drive from the old historic mining town of Warren and the Guard station there, where we are based. The last ten miles, descending into the canyon, are a rough and steep single dirt lane with occasional pullouts. It's a first-gear drive down and takes an hour.

When I catch my first glimpse of the South Fork Canyon, of the Salmon River Break country, my imagination expands and yearns to explore the space. I wonder about the animals that live here, and about the earlier Native Americans who inhabited these lands. Anglo and Chinese miners all called the canyon home in historical times, aiding in the removal of these first people. *I don't know enough history!*

That there is a wild river in the canyon's floor amplifies my eagerness to see and learn more about the area, as it reminds me of my transformative Middle Fork adventures. I strain to see the river from the pickup's passenger window seat. We're driving along the river, which lays off to our left, off the driver's side. I glimpse a river swollen with spring runoff. White water waves. Green with cold. But I see through its clean, clear depths to the rocks in its bed.

Seeing the guard station, my imagination flowers with dreams of what it might be like to live there. The log cabin is an old historic Forest Service one, sitting quietly alone on a bench, forty yards or so above the river. I cannot imagine a more Waldenesque setting, with large ponderosa pines on the hillside above. It's seventy-odd miles back to McCall. I figure it's a three-hour drive. Remote. Wild country. Hot. "River-breaks country," they call it. People speak of the wildfire potential in that country with a quiet, if not fearful, respect.

After my first trip down, I make every effort to be on any crew doing work there. I do not hesitate to say, "Yes," when asked if I might consider heading up a two-man assignment there the following spring. It is a dream come true. I can't believe my luck!

Settling into the South Fork Guard Station assignment is like finding myself swimming in a world of unbounded natural beauty. It is a kind of homecoming for my soul, a womb in nature. I am immersed in clean and wild air, soil, trees, and rocks, and getting paid for the baptism. I am in heaven. Insulated, except by Forest Service radio contact, from civilization's day-to-day distractions. *I cannot believe my damn luck. Getting paid to live in a place of such isolated beauty.*

Something within intuitively knows that slowing down life is key to my personal transformation, and finally, it feels there is at last place and time enough for just this medicine. Time for just catching my breath, and for catching up with myself from life's challenges and changes. Time for exploring and settling into the mysteries of who I might truly be, and for integrating and releasing the pains of the past.

Plus, I get paid to sweat! Yeah, I like the pleasures of feeling strong in hard work, feeling muscles stretch and strain, and enduring tasks, like running the chainsaw or cutting a fire line, or hiking and clearing trails.

If it sounds like I was some kind of man's man here, I was not. I felt both insecure about my physical powers and confident of them. I am eager, though, to prove myself in a world of laboring men, and hungry for their acceptance and company as well. What is difficult for me is the bureaucratic equivalent of occasional orders to dig a hole for an unknown purpose but of specific dimensions, waiting, and then being told to fill it in because someone somewhere changed their mind. There are regulations for everything, with little room for personal creativity or initiative.

"Good enough for government work," is the occasional joke as we wrap up such a job, coming from men forbidden to use their own minds for a job at hand. Being on the South Fork frees me from most of that. I am in charge—of me and a crew of one other man. We are our own helitack team, with a chopper stationed up the canyon away, upstream yet from Williams Peak Lookout, at Krassel. Our job is to clean and fix the place up, patrol the roads and one primitive campground along the river, and take care of the lookout on Pilot Peak, all while waiting for a lightning strike with our name on it. But the common days are ones when the excitement and adrenaline of flames do not call.

These are the days of listening deeper and deeper into nature as a teacher and mirror, somehow, of my own being. The South Fork River becomes a daily studied presence in my life, one that endures beyond my continuing clumsy relationship attempts with women.

I sit on a rock under the tall pines beside the river and listen to the dancing waters sing. I listen for the possible reemergence of the voices-without-words I heard on the cliff face along the Middle Fork.

Even on days of stillness, the river's moving waters subtly stir the air against my cheek. One day, when the light is uniquely just right, I see tire-sized donut-shaped rainbows, suspended just above the water as if barely held by gravity. They bounce and float playfully along downriver. The river seduces my heart and there is a resonance of oneness between it, the blood in my veins, and even the water in my cellular tissues. That I, too, am water, is a spiraling realization coming home like snowflakes pulled by gravity.

"Teach me," I pray to the river, knowing this is a request that will require a somatic-soul-spirit listening deeper than any known to me.

I study how water conforms its flow to whatever surface it meets— answers these encounters with songs of whirlpools, eddies, and liquid pouring over and around rocks in a dance with refracted sunlight and the vanilla smells of ponderosa pines.

I bring my worn and dog-eared book, the *Tao Te Ching*, by the ancient Chinese philosopher, Lao Tsu, to the river with me. His voice adds to the symphony of sensations that wash through my body-mind. The opening stanzas undercut and challenge the fundamentalistic theology of my childhood and become a mantra I hear repeated in the river's songs.

> The Tao (way) that can be told is not the eternal Tao.
> The name that can be named is not the eternal Name.
> —Lao Tsu, *Tao Te Ching*, verse 1

It's like the power of naming shapes perception, imparts an illusionary sense of knowledge or of control even. And it's also how we communicate. Yet might language be a Tree-of-Knowledge kind of power, for good or for unconscious evil? Maybe because we hinge our identities on our beliefs, our stories of good and evil?

Even as I think this, an image comes to mind of two armies fighting against each other in righteous war, each with God on *their* side. *It's like the Crusades, Christians and Muslims. Yet, the mystery that can be named is not the true One!*

My mind wanders into the question of what it is to be a man. The strong standalone John Wayne tobacco-chewing, whisky-drinking, fighting-man image of masculinity, untouched by emotional vulnerability. I think of masculine models of leadership, supporting social structures of self-interest with clear and concise decision-making independent of the cost of others, lives or not. I think of President Nixon and the self-sustaining military industry, feeding on the cultivation of fear.

Yet in Lao Tsu, I read:

> Under heaven, nothing is more soft and yielding than water.
> Yet for attacking the solid and strong, nothing is better.
> —Lao Tsu, *Tao Te Ching*, verse 78

A quote often attributed to George Washington Carver comes to mind. "Anything will talk to you if you love it enough," also ripples through my system as a reminder to listen deeply, with yet more attention. *Teach me Water*, I pray again.

And the river does talk to me, and I with it. So too, I talk with the neighboring creeks and springs, the trees, animals, soil, and skies of pregnant storms. I spend uncounted hours and days in presence and companionship with River, its waters on its way to the ocean. Its waters, I come to realize, already are ocean, the way raindrops that feed the river are river, before they ever flow in its bed.

My tattered copy of *Siddhartha*, by Hermann Hesse, flows into my heart and veins like water coming home. I read of the pilgrim, Prince Siddhartha, who has given up his wealth and worldly powers in search of spiritual enlightenment. He comes to a river that is perceived by most travelers as an impediment to their journeys. But the ferryman he encounters, and the river, change his life. For as the ferryman says, "It was the river that taught me to listen, and it will teach you as well. It knows everything, the river, and one can learn anything from it." (Hesse 2008, 89)

Teach me of life, I ask of River, time and again. *Teach me to let go of all my pain and sorrow and grieving. Teach me to fully embrace and to love myself*, I pray of Water. And when I find myself in flow or stillness, as Water, I begin to find my prayers fulfilled.

"This land made fish. There used to be so many salmon spawning here you could walk across the river on their backs." Clay spits a juicy Red Man onto the ground for punctuation.

I wanted to believe him. It was no secret what the dams elsewhere were doing to the anadromous fish runs. And I had learned that several years back the Forest Service had allowed intense clear-cutting along the banks of the South Fork, up above Krassel. Apparently, heavy rains in subsequent years made a mockery of their stewardship through repeated revelations of natural laws. Massive loads of silt washed into the river, scoured, and destroyed the salmon spawning beds. It was an ecological disaster if you were a salmon, or say a bear, eagle, dragonfly nymph, or a human living off the land's prior diversity and abundance.

It makes no sense to me that clear-cuts are still allowed, except they be driven by the power of money. Can people not see what greed and short-term thinking are doing to the forests and rivers we all love?

But now I let different imaginations flood my brain—images of silvery-hued colors full of life and water, jumping and splashing, spawning a bursting of semen and eggs in a glorious re-genesis of life. For moments of awe, I see the river below us thick with fish. Mystery. So, filling the ancient river thirty yards away, I can walk across the river as I step by step on their liquid backs.

But such visions can be fragile and hard to hold on to, like the fish themselves. "Oh, come on, Clay. Seriously?"

Clay looks me dead in the eye, from under his dirty worn felt cowboy hat, and challenges me to disbelief. "That's a fact," Clay says, and spits again.

I swallow my tobacco juice and shake my head with sorrow for what is lost. For what I, what no one, will ever see again.

Clay is our closest and only neighbor down on the South Fork, the one summer he was there when I was, out of my two there. I hear he has a place around McCall too, though I never run into him in town. I figure Clay to be at least in his seventies and he can sure garden.

Clay grows the most abundant garden I've ever seen, certainly enough to keep a few families in vegetables. Clearly, Clay believes what he often tells me, "Growing food is the most valuable thing a man can do." He always follows up this statement with a punctuating silence. Stringing his thoughts together in the slow way he works his garden, the way he selectively lets the spring's irrigation water run between chosen rows of crops, Clay's stories and his decades of living on this land are released gently into the patient pool of quiet between us.

"There used to be maybe two hundred people living down here in this canyon, back in the depression. Back in the depression," he repeats himself as though it improves the focus of his memory. "Living off the land too! Shoot, there wasn't anything else to live off of back then! Weren't any jobs."

Clay and I stand looking out over his treasure of food. He leans on his hoe. Fresh clean earth soils his worn blue jeans and faded denim shirt. Who knows when they were last washed, or when he last shaved? Although his salt and pepper stubble never grows beyond that. I never see him without his pearl-handled revolver pistol in a holster slung low on his hip, the way he wears his jeans too.

"For the rattlesnakes," he says of the gun. "That, and there's people out there that want my gold. You never know when they might ambush me and then they'd torture me to make me talk. Put splinters under my fingernails... They'd try to make me tell 'em where I hide it. Shoot, I got gold dust stashed in lots of places! I don't want 'em catching me."

Clay always stops himself in mid-sentence with pauses when he notices himself talking about his gold stashes. But he'll talk about the way things used to be on the South Fork and his garden till my ears sprout green. Out of our rambling conversations comes his occasional repeated question, as if he hasn't asked it of me before.

"What are you going to do with your life?" he asks. Without waiting for an answer, he advises me, in light of his own Great Depression era life experience. "Growing food is the most important job a man can do. We went hungry, back in the depression. I had my wife and two kids. We wouldn't have made it without poaching. Shoot, everybody did it."

"Did you see the bear up by your place this morning?" he asks.

"No, I didn't. Was he over by the apple trees?"

"Yeah." Silence often descends into our conversations more than the words. They are the slow exchanges of folks who do not see many other people around. The talk, in fact, grows out of the silences, like trees growing out of a crack in a boulder, or Clay's garden growing day by day, rooted in the rich black soil he nourishes.

Clay's shack sits on a rock shelf, fifteen feet or so right above a quiet pool of water at the river's edge below. It's his patented gold claim that allows him to have his place on the river where he does.

I never ask, but wonder if he occasionally might throw a fishing line right out the west window into the quiet pool below. The idyllic setting provides contrast to the short and worn dirt path leading to his front door, past a wire fence and faded white wooden gate with an equally dilapidated sign. A similar one adorns a roughly built shed in the back. "No trespassing! Protected by bullet, dynamite, and explosives!"

I'm over for coffee one morning when a grouse flies in the open north window. It lands on the arm of a ratty stuffed chair. Perhaps it is my imagination that makes the bird appear confused as it looks around its new surroundings. But it soon jumps to the floor and wanders easily about a bit. Then the grouse flies out the open door. We sit in the two old wooden chairs at the scarred scrap wood table, in front of the window it flew through, drinking our cowboy coffee in comfortable silence. Neither of us ever says a word about the bird.

"I've got gold fever," he says. "I dream about gold. About finding it." And then he tells me again, "We went hungry during the depression. Growing food is the most important thing a man can do. What are you going to do with your life?" he asks again, as if for the first time.

I do not know how to tell Clay of the inner response his question elicits. *I want to let my life grow out of the soil of living, for it to emerge from the earthiness of living the way the tall old ponderosas in the neighborhood do. If I had planned or predicted what I was going to do with my life, it never would have been this grand. Discovering this is like finding gold. It is like finding gold because it suggests that perhaps I can indeed trust this experience of life—that there is, inside, a deep self of being that can be trusted.*

I also increasingly suspect the universe itself is somehow reciprocally responsive to my emotions and thinking. But to trust in such a worldview—can I really be that powerful? Is this just more of your crazy thinking, Larry?

This is no small thing! Such a trust might make a person the way a landscape makes fish, the way fish can weave diversity and landscapes of bears, otters, beavers, snakes, eagles, osprey, salamanders, hatches of insects, and people. Perhaps this is the original sin humanity yet perpetrates—separating ourselves from the landscape our very being is grounded in as if we do not belong, as if this is not our home, as if it is not a mirror we peer into, as if the observer can be separated from the observed. No wonder, for some of us, a deep trust of self can be hard to come by.

I'm fortunate indeed. A broken compass is a good thing to discover. Same as with a map that does not match reality. And to learn both are in error is itself a kind invitation for birth into a new life.

There is a cairn placed in the mind of my heart in honor of and as a reminder of what it can be for a worldview to change. It is similar in ways to the impact the Blue Baby continues to have on my life. This memory is of hiking off to a two-man fire to the nearest backcountry road. It would not have been more than a few miles. Our Forest Service green canvas backpacks are loaded and our hands full of firefighting gear, including chainsaw, shovels, and Pulaskis with their sharp blades wrapped and tied in canvas, bedrolls, and water. We dump leftover saw gas and oil before starting the hike out.

We follow a ridge line down a way, then drop off toward a creek where we can intersect a forest road. This is not nearly as exciting as getting picked up off the fire by helicopter, but it happens, depending upon logistical circumstances. The Lodgepole pine timber we hike amidst is thick, stunted in growth, and skeleton-like.

The species is known for its *dog hair* like stands, but this one is so thick and close together it feels to me to be a forest of mutual strangulation. Claustrophobia settles into me like darkness in a crowded room when the lights go out unexpectedly. Getting a suntan in that near unbroken shade would require exercise, chasing rare shafts of light. Tall gray-black and thin-barked trees of a foot diameter both stand and lie chaotically scattered everywhere. *It is a tangled maze in here!*

Uprooted and broken trees lie upon compatriots like stick matches spilled from a box by an invisible hand. Waist-high logs lie upon others, propped into varying angles; their stability is hinged upon one or more others. To walk on the patchy forest floor, a tree-branch-littered carpet of thick dry brown pine needles, is impracticable. We walk balanced upon one log until a more inviting one crosses our path, going generally in our desired direction. It is a meandering zigzag hike, with us occasionally balancing higher off the ground than preferred. This makes for slow, difficult, and sometimes hazardous progress.

An awareness descends upon me like a depressing rain. *I haven't seen any sign of wildlife. No deer, elk, bear, or even rabbit scat. No rubbings. No squirrels scolding us, objecting to our presence. No birds flitting from twig to branch. No bird song. No Gambel oak or other brush inserts their greenery onto the shadowy forest floor. And most of the trees are dead!*

The ghostly silence is punctuated only by the occasional eerie creak of one tree fallen, caught in the crotch of another, straining against its captor, moved by a fey breeze from another world.

There is nothing for critters to eat in here. Big critters can't get around in here any easier than we can. This is a mess. It's a monoculture. No diversity. One species growing like a parasite turned in on itself. All the life is gone out of this area. This is a skeleton forest! All bones and no flesh—no claw, fur, or feather. No diversity.

I'm hiking that day with Jerry. He is a tall, lanky fellow with an easy-going attitude, and a few years younger than me. He has a couple of seasons up on me with the Forest Service though. In my first year working out of McCall, we are often partnered and he generously shares his own developing knowledge of Forest Service ways with me. My memory is of us, at one point, walking parallel logs, opposite each other, and fifteen or twenty feet apart. My experience of the place just blurts out.

"This place needs to burn, Jerry!"

"Don't it though," he comes back. "It's way overdue."

"Yeah, and it'll burn way too hot when it does. The fuel buildup in here is incredible. This is a firestorm waiting to happen."

"Sure seems that way." Jerry is not prone to exaggeration. He attaches himself to detail and fact as if they are sequential stepping-stones in a creek he wants to cross. "Course, the irony here is this lodgepole needs fire to open its cones up, so the seeds can spill. Takes something like a 120-degree temperature to make 'em open. It's called *serotinous*, I think. It allows the seeds to remain viable for decades even, lying around waiting for a fire to come through."

I feel stunned as I let this fact in. It's a fascinating fire adaptive detail and strategy I was ignorant of—that some forest species need fire for their health or even life cycle. Did no one tell Smokey of this, back when war was declared against all forest fires, after the Great Fire of 1910?

Later, I learn of the fire adaptive strategy of other trees, such as ponderosa pines and Douglas firs. They develop a thick protective insulating bark, of perhaps several inches in depth, that actually contains fire retardant capacities. This can allow a ground fire to come through a grove, burn the smaller fuels before they build up, and thin other shade-loving species and smaller trees that otherwise would compete with or even strangle these magnificent old-growth giants.

On this day, however, I glimpse into the depths of my ecological illiteracy, how ignorant I am of the ways of nature. I suddenly sense fire as a great actor at play within nature's realms of creation and destruction, carrying the god-like powers of each. I sense landscape scale complexities interweaving variables such as altitude, moisture, sun, and shade, that bring life and diversity to western forests.

The Social Work education introduced me to systems thinking and the interconnectivity of social issues like poverty, social justice, and generational social inequity. However, it is during my Forest Service time that I become enchanted with the ideas of Living Systems thinking, with learning to see into ecological wholeness. Writers and thinkers like Gregory Bateson, with his *Steps to an Ecology of Mind*, reinforce my growing sense that of our loss of reference to nature's operating principles, what I might now call *the eros of life for itself*, is the primary cause of personal and escalating social problems.

It's like, by learning to see the interconnectivity of the forest, I'm learning to better see what it is to be human. To see my own face in the forest, so to speak. I'm more like the forest than different. I'm not separate after all. What a gift of healing!

Ecological questions of identity begin reverberating in my body and dreams. Questions like: *What does it mean to live with fire in my belly, to live life with passion, change, and transformation, as givers and takers of life? What is it to make an ally of the unknowns of a descending chaos that will burn away social constructions of*

identity? What is it to know Fire as a living presence, an energy, a dynamic sacred process that redefines boundaries, deepens diversity, and from which new life and identity can come?

What if I play with the idea of my hatred and anger, and righteous judgmentalism as expressions of fire? And love too! Is not the fire of the Sun the same fire that digests the food in my belly, food that itself also once digested Sun's fire, and now passes that energy on to me? And so the Sun actually lives in every cell of my body—through the biological flows of metabolism!

Surely it is an ailment within my civilized self that does not know, respect, and honor the God of Fire living within, as much as without! And life and death are no more opposites than are creation and destruction, than male and female, light and dark. They are all expressions of a deeper oneness, out of which these polarities arise and manifest the material world.

And I—I contain them all.

And one day, lying yet decades into the future from these early glimpses into the ecological self, it will be the fire adaptive strategies of yet another tree that will further transform my identity and worldview. It is, for me, indeed all an internal resurrection of the sacred.

What More Theology

Tell me please, dear soul,
when you walk upon Earth
do the soles of your feet
touch your mother with your heart?

And when you walk with this lover
do you not find pleasure and joy
in caressing her with your every step?

Do you not walk deliberately
like the tortoise
offering prayers of gratitude
for the gifts of air and water and soil
for food and the companionship of kinship
with the rooted ones
four-legged and winged and swimmers
and crawling ones too?

Do you not nourish your life
your very spirit with this loving embrace
of sole and soil and soul?

Does not this embrace
bring alive within
eyes and mind and heart innately drawn
to mystery and curiosity, beauty and belonging?

Tell me please, dear one,
does this not make you a practitioner
of the world's oldest religion,
the original religion of love
of awe and wonder too,
the Mother religion
of all religions?

Now please, tell me too,
what more theology
might anyone ever need?

Chapter 9

THE ONCE AND FUTURE HUMAN

Is there more to the world than the cultural mind reveals to me? And might some of this unseen nature of the universe even be reciprocally sensitive to the attitudes, manners, and vibrations of my engagement with it? I feel utterly deceived and betrayed by the fundamentalist beliefs of my inheritance, and then again by my own adoption of those beliefs. Now I want to know if I can trust Life not to betray me! And can I trust myself, my own body and mind and dreams—not to betray myself?

Such questions haunt me and lead to explorations of my inner world equal to those of the re-mapping of outer Nature as a sacred landscape. I am living in unknown and tricky territories where direct experience becomes even more valuable as I compost inherited beliefs that solidify identities into objects, rather than relationships. Yet I also want to be sensitive to not creating, out of desire, illusions of reciprocal responsiveness between the cosmos and this self that do not independently exist outside my skull.

But will I be able to see what I am not looking for? Like, perhaps, a Kingdom of the Father spread upon the earth, as Jesus said, that men do not see?

I need to feel my identity and life are in alignment with the true Ground of Being upon which I walk and within which I exist.

Ted is a quiet, reflective, and six-foot-plus young man with a physique that leaves my skinny-body self-image jealous. In his early twenties, Ted has a love relationship with the earth that we each recognize and respect in the other. I'm quick to grab an empty bar stool next to him one evening, eager to hear his version of a story another buddy recently told me.

"So, Ted. Jim told me what you did with the rattlesnake down at the South Fork."

"Oh, that!" Ted says with a laugh. "The poor snake was just coiled up and sleeping in a back corner of the barn. They grabbed a couple of shovels and were going to kill it. I didn't think that was right, so I picked it up and threw it in their direction. I didn't really throw it at them. I just wanted it to at least have a fighting chance by making it angry, so I woke it up."

"They both ran right out the door when I did that. You should have seen 'em!"

We're laughing hard together, as Ted finishes his story. And I'm thinking, *What a difference worldview makes in how we meet the world!*

"Well, here's to the snake," I say as I raise my glass for a toast. "Next round is on me!"

Ted will go on to become a Smokejumper and bail out of flying airplanes, while I will bail out of the Forest Service several years later.

Meanwhile, Ted is the first and one of the few people I ever risked sharing the story of my encounter with the Earth Spirits. We'd flown into Las Vegas, NV, a few days before and then bussed to the base camp for what was quickly becoming a large project fire, meaning there were already several crews on scene with more coming. Ted and I are part of a Twenty-man Payette NF crew riding out as close to the wildfire as they can get us, in the back of a National Guard large open-bedded truck.

It is still early morning as we are bounced and jarred around while the driver navigates the rough and dusty two-track. Some of the men sit in silence with their private thoughts. Others joke and banter the way people who work closely together will.

Fighting fires made for hard living and good friends. Men I liked, respected, and enjoyed being on a fire line with. In this way, the project fires were social gatherings of sorts, especially when the adrenaline runs and you're counting your overtime and hazard pay. But if it was a big fire, I wanted out of there when it came to mop-up. The fire was contained by then and the work just gets real down and dirty, and boring. No more adrenalin or hazard pay, and it takes one away from a possible lightning strike with your name on it.

It was a great world to be in, particularly given my questioning the make-up of reality. The depths of my questions and inner reflectivity require a living landscape supportive of living centered not out of my head but as deeply incarnated and rooted into this body as possible.

The feral world of the trees, dirt, rocks, and animals is real for me, tangible and navigable, like dangerous hard work, blisters, and sweat. But at night? I wonder about my dreams. I often experience lucidity, the feeling of being awake during dreams, knowing I am dreaming. Sometimes I wake exhausted, from all the battles, the fighting of dragons, and the lucid encounters with wise old men, or women, who teach me about the ways of the world, or of the forest. But I also love flying in my dreams. I learn that if I can become conscious of my breath in a dream, I can levitate and fly at will. It is great fun!

But all this dreaming leaves me wandering amidst inquiries into which world is a dream and which is not. The more I play with my dreams, the more they play with me, and the more it feels there is a continuous thread of awareness, day and night.

This leaves me with what feels to be an other-than-normal life, and one where I feel yet like a neophyte in navigating the darkness and shadows of my nights and days. Having time on the job to work with my dreams, to live with them and play them repeatedly, akin to the way I'd work over a tree's stump hole on a small fire, feels like an honoring of the light and dark within, of the known and the unknowns.

Sometimes a fire will burn out an old tree stump—decades of squirrel pinecone debris build up a kindling-like soft and spongy-to-walk-on duff several feet thick, perfect for nourishing an underground charcoal fire. When the duff, stump, and root system are smoldering into charcoal and ash, there might be a waist-deep hole and a lot of hot-root tunnels and yards of deep territory to dig up and around in for hours. "Cold to touch," is the rule.

Returning to it again and again, after working in other areas, your bare skin gets to know every dimensional inch of it, like working a dream gift over.

I spend time getting into each of the dream characters, try to see the experience from their point of view. It is a meditative and reflective composting of life, and of dreams, which continues to inform and change who I am.

Sometimes in my dreams, however, I feel like I encounter other consciousnesses, like actual other entities who have an autonomous presence apart from the generation of my own personal unconscious dream material.

I do not know how to mesh these experiences with reality—at least with Reality 101, as I learned it in church and school. I am sure I'd test loony on some psychological profile.

I wonder about my sanity. But I take refuge in my body: the way it knows how to walk amidst rattlesnakes on a narrow, steep, rocky trail where one side drops a hundred feet to the river below. It knows how to breathe and find a rhythm of putting one foot in front of the other for miles through the forest. It knows how to place each step onto Earth as though caressing her with my heart and to be reciprocally caressed by her as well.

I love that my bodily senses have awakened and know how to sense into the world with a soft peripheral listening, like being penetrated by the distant and soft sounds of the river, or how to taste the smells of vanilla as sunlight streams through the tall golden barked ponderosa pines. I am enamored with allowing in the deep silence that speaks so loudly, saying, "Stop! Be still! Listen!"

I listen. I feel nature teaching me to be ever more in love with life. I am in love with mystery too, exploring it without attaching myself to beliefs that nail down my identity, my concretized vision of reality.

These experiences of extended time in nature, what will become years of sleeping under an orchestra of stars, feed my soul and spirit. They give me reason to live, this savoring of the curiosity and awe and wonder I now swim in.

The mystery of Bear is part of this and still plays within me too, informing my breathing like an awakening seed in soil. Clearly, I had touched another consciousness and been touched by a non-human sentient presence as well. For some brief eternity of time, I was Bear. That ancestral hunters called them, "Bear People," I now understood. Bears have bear-consciousness and individual personality. *They are a people, a tribe, a clan, a species of a different consciousness than ours, but kin nevertheless. And to all humans, whether a person knows them as family or as fear. Not unlike snakes, apparently.*

I sought the luck of seeing Bear in the forest and knew Ted would feel blessed by such as well. He still carries a certain resonance of wildness about himself. It is this signature of his presence that allows me to risk a conversation into the dream world as we each try to let the dark green National Guard truck's bucking-around ride through us like reeds in a current of water.

Just considering whether to risk sharing my dreams with Ted, I can't help but remember asking Dad, once, if he ever remembers his dreams.

"No." He pauses, and then continues, "I don't dream."

And the sharing of these dreams feels like sacred, intimate territory, so I began tentatively. "Say, Ted. Do you pay attention to your dreams?"

"Yeah, sometimes."

"I had these two last night that blew me away. They were so real. Sometimes I wonder if the dream world isn't as real as this one. Do you know what I mean?"

"Yeah. It's like that Carlos Castaneda stuff. I try to *be awake* in my dreams sometimes, but it's hard. I've tried watching my hand like he talks about, but I can never hold its image. How about you?" (Castaneda 1993).

"Yeah, I find focusing on the hand thing hard too. Can I share a dream from last night?

"Sure. Long as we got time."

"Well, in the first one, I'm walking down a country road, going to a friend's house. I walk up to the door, knock, and am let in. Then I see myself sitting at a round table with three other people. That's when I become aware I am dreaming. I'm startled by the vivid realization. It wasn't like being in most dreams. Everything is so real, so tangible."

"Then I find that breathing consciously brings the situation and environment into greater clarity. I realize I have a rare opportunity to seize this moment and begin a conversation with the other folks at the table."

"So," I begin, "I am dreaming. Is anyone else here dreaming too? Everybody looks at me funny, at first. Then, one by one, there is a sort of dawning awareness on each of their faces. And, one by one, each of them acknowledges they are dreaming too. We get caught up in the excitement of all of us being awake together in the same dream. Then, of course, we decide we have to figure out a way to reconnect and confirm our experience. You know, on the daylight side of life."

"That's when I lost it. It was a simple realization that addresses or phone numbers or even names were far too complex to hold on to. Then it's like this awareness spreads among us: it has to be a certain sparkle of recognition, a knowing look, in another's eyes."

Ted sits next to me with a big smile on his face. He says nothing, so I just push ahead. "Can I tell you the next one?"

"Sure."

"Well, after that dream, I have the distinct feeling of re-entering, of settling back into my body. It's sort of like floating down into it, from above. I feel awed by the dream and re-play the details in my mind, you know, trying to stay in that half-awake kind of place. That's when I hear something stirring, just a ways up the hill behind me, near a clump of bushes. At first, I thought it was that guy who likes yelling to wake us up this morning. I felt relief when I realized it wasn't him. The guy irritates me. Then I felt afraid."

"There was this unsettled *stir* going on. It was like a subtle wind rustling around in the brush and grass. Then I hear this whispering begin, and it builds into more of a kind of commotion."

"I feel like I was wide awake," I continue. "I become conscious of the subtle lie of the ground under my back, and the quiet all around where our bags are laid. I calm myself by breathing. I know I am awake. I can see the stars. But I wonder if I might be dreaming too. It was the weirdest thing."

Ted continues his easy-listening gaze into the dust kicked up by our passing. His quiet smile speaks just enough that I know he is listening, despite my feeling a bit awkward at the time taken to share my story. He waits patiently when I pause, so I just continue.

"Then all the rustling around stops. Suddenly. In this space of deep quiet that follows, I sense a decision reached. Someone has been chosen, and I have this clarity that allows me to know what is happening."

"Several Earth Spirts have come together. It is their eager mumblings among themselves that alert me to their presence. Then I remember, I had sensed some of them during the day yesterday when we were working on the line. But I hadn't recognized them— as themselves. And they had been watching my awake dreaming."

"So now this appointed spirit comes slowly forward. He distinctly gives me time to get out of my body and stand up. Then we are like these two respectful spirits, standing comfortably close, face to face. We stand before each other, looking with an easy gaze into each other's eyes. I perceive him to be about my age. He is dressed in buckskins, but without clothes, too. I am aware this image of him I see is projected for my comfort. He gives me time to feel at ease with him, then asks a question."

"Who are you that travels in your sleep awake?"

"I am startled by his question. Then, I'm suddenly aware of all the spirits, like a waiting audience, behind him. I consider his question—take time to breathe consciously and allow it in. It feels like an important moment and question, you know? Then I decide to assert myself, and spontaneously answer, for lack of anything more creative—'I...am me!' That's what I said. And that's the dream. But both dreams were so real. Makes me wonder what's *real*, and what's just imagination, ya know?"

Ted acknowledges his understanding with a release of concentration and a wide, knowing smile that sparkles in his eyes. Men are already unloading off the back of the truck. We each take our turn in sequence, jump down, and more dust flies about us as our boots hit the ground. We pick a tool out of the pile before gathering briefly as a team of men wearing hard hats, fire-resistant Nomex yellow shirts and green pants. Emergency fire shelters in their red packs are strapped to our waists, and quart water bottles ride on either side of that. Radios crackle with the activity of other crews coming off or going onto the line. We begin our hike through the rough high desert country to the fire. I take notice of the men I work with, and the surrounding landscape, through different eyes—eyes of awakened curiosity, inner eyes looking to sense into what is that I have been conditioned to deny or ignore.

I keep my vision peripherally aware, more softly focused through the day, and try to see into the scrub forest with a heightened depth of perception and curiosity. Might I see one of last night's spirits? Though none appear to me, I still wonder what presence it is I sense in a subtle shift or stirring of a breeze, or a momentary, barely noticeable, change of temperature, the unseen but peripherally sensed movement, or in the settled dignity and quietness around a particular gathering of rock and brush.

Both dreams, like geographical places of emotional significance throughout one's life, continue to work their influence and inform my living for years. And years. Still. For, of course, from one perspective, this Forest Spirit is me, asking just this of myself: "Who are you that travels in your dreams awake?"

What I did not share with Ted is the Earth Spirit's response to my reply to his question.

"We will call you, Spirit Tracker."

I could not have then shared that I would come to recognize this as a naming of a core soul purpose for me: to track the journey of my awakening but also to track the collective human soul's journey into forgetting, and into *re*membering.

How is one to carry such through life, anyway? The sense that... there even is a soul? Whatever that might be. And that one's soul might have purpose and meaning intrinsic to itself, independent of extrinsic social identity and structures. Too intimately, I already knew of and feared the capacity for my beliefs to follow emotional need, regardless of external facts.

It is now roughly fifty years later, as I write this, that I can name these two dreams as invitations to live into the awakening of my mythic eyes and heart.

It is perhaps five years later, and the winter before I will go on the fire lookout come summer. I sit and sense into the presence of the psychedelic psilocybin mushrooms before partaking of them. They break into chewy bits in my mouth and taste like... dried fungus. Just a bit gritty, like fine soil. One must want the effect to eat them in this intimate way, but one also quickly learns the taste is not noxious. It is simply fleshy soil.

But the mushrooms like to be eaten, as I experience them anyway. And my experience is they welcome the subsequent communication between us as much as I. It is not without reason the mushrooms were known as the "flesh of the gods" to the indigenous people when the Spanish arrived in the New World. When I reverently ate the flesh of Christ during communion service in church, I never came to the experience with the anticipation, fear, trembling, and awe that, over time, I learned to approach mushrooms with.

My first introduction to mushrooms was as a party drug, ingested for the sensory high they brought on, for the way they loosened me up. They allowed me to explore body movement with dance, something I was still too emotionally constricted to do straight. As a party drug, they let me drink more and longer into the night. And making love on those low doses was particularly good, with the heightened sensorial acuity.

But it is a higher dosage of mushrooms I want to explore on this night. At higher doses of ingestion, mystical states of awe, wonder, and knowing descend into bodily presence. Terrifying experiences can manifest themselves as well, and at a time when one cannot distinguish reality from hallucination. That's why some sense of fear and trembling denotes a healthy respect for the medicine's powers—a nightmare on psychedelics is one amplified beyond imagination.

Even the awe and wonder can be of such magnitude as to leave one uncomfortably alone and disoriented in the universe or with an ego inflated with grandiosity. They seem to create space for the unknown and forbidden territories within to emerge—and this is just the reality I want to explore.

I eat the mushrooms with intention and purpose, seeking to focus on the direction of their revelatory powers. I want to explore my relationship with women—more specifically, on my relationship with pain, pleasure, and women.

I desire to better understand the women of my many failed relationships. I hunger to feel what it is to perceive the world through feminine eyes. I have such a hard time with women, accepting either their rejection or allowing in their love. I do not know how to be in a relationship with them. It is painful.

There is no escape from my loneliness and horniness. I think about women and sex with about the same frequency that I breathe. I spend a frustrated Idaho winter-week counting women I've slept with. It is a way of trying to accrue self-worth, of trying to remind myself that I do have value and worth, or else all those women would never have slept with me. Right?

I stop counting at a hundred. *This is most of 'em anyway, remembered by occasion if not by name.*

It is this constellation of energies I carry into the medicine journey as I seek to better understand my relational dynamics with women and the depths of my cravings for them. I've been experimenting with sculpting faces out of leather, using thin light-grade oak-tanned cowhide. I find I can use a spray bottle to wet it with a water-alcohol solution, helping it dry more quickly while maintaining a pliable and moldable material capable of holding form.

I stand at a table, massage the leather with love and anticipation, stretch and pull at it to loosen it up. I invite some sculptural image to emerge but do not yet see it in my eye. It will have to be sensual. Sensuous. Nipples and folds of leather take and lose shape in the creative process of hands at play, looking for meaningful form.

I breathe—consciously. Intentionally. Long, slow, deep inhalations. Long, slow, deep exhalations. These are interspersed with a pause, to be with the silence in-between breaths, all while I play with the skin-like leather. My fingers love the leather's sensuality. This wet, moist, pliable material. Memories of all the women in my life flood through me: Mom, with the broken-record refrain of "Don't forget whose kid you are." But then the faces and bodies and experiences roll into my system like women still living inside. There's Lisa, Fey, Sarah, Jennifer, Terry, Diane...

Each are distinctive signatures of feminine presence and energy in my life. Each with her own history, personality, and sensuality of skin and flesh. Each finding her path into my heart's softening, opening—maybe this time—and then the emotional pain, wounding, and bleeding. The "How can you just throw my love away?" and "I feel sorry for you. I may be insecure, but you are afraid to let love in...." I am deep in the altered state of medicine's spell. It flows in my blood and amplifies the fires of passion and desire.

I am a pilgrim, forging my own path into the unknown as I stand at the table, remembering passion's seductions and my heart's frustrated desires, the loves and losses of my life. I work the leather with knees lightly bent to better sense the aliveness in my legs and play with shifting balance from one foot to the other. It is a dance of sensing the soles of my feet connect to Earth. Roots grow down and deep into the Mother.

And with each breath in, I intend the conscious drawing up of this sacred feminine energy into my body. My studies into yoga are elemental, for I distrust spiritual teachers and maps of all traditions. *Kundalini*, however, I remember as a name given to this life force I seek to explore. And *chakras*, seven supposed esoteric subtle body energy centers, beginning from the root at the base of the spine, then the sacrum as an emotional and sexual center, rising to the solar plexus, the heart, throat, third eye, and crown chakra, or pure awareness.

My hope is that if I can awaken this feminine aspect of Kundalini's serpent-like powers within, this will grant me a window into understanding the feminine without and within. My studies suggest it is a latent spiritual force awaiting awakening, *like a coiled snake*, residing down in the lower pelvic area. The idea, as I understand it, is to bring this life force up the spine consciously with each breath, opening into each of the next six chakras on its way.

So, I play with the leather and the breath, feel energy rise up through my roots, up my lightly trembling legs and swirl around my lower pelvis, and try to sense my spinal tip. Feeling a sensation of building energy here is easy enough, as I'm horny and flashing through all the lovemaking of my years. My sense of being grounded, of growing roots, awakens here. But can I pull the energy up my spine? Build it? Experience its transformation, its character, in each of these supposed chakras?

Memories of lovemaking wash over me in a flood of desires, of women, passion, sensuality, and hurt. This adds fuel to the fire of the building energy. So do the mantra-like refrain of the questions I swim in: *Who are you, woman? What is your essence in the world? Can I experience your energy, the feminine? See the world as you do? May I see your true face?*

I breathe in slowly and deeply, almost as if sucking on a straw, pulling an almost-electrical energy up my spine, into my belly just below the navel. I let it sink back down with a deep conscious and full exhalation. Then I bring even more energy up with the next inhalation. I can feel some of the energy wanting to flow further up my spine, but I try to concentrate on building the intensity of charge here before moving on. All the lovemaking and lust of my life co-join to draw energy from the Earth into my roots and legs and build intensity in the pelvic area.

When it seems that I can indeed feel an open conduit of energy flowing freely between these first and second chakra areas, I draw this energy yet higher up my spine, into the solar plexus. Again, there is the internal focus upon opening, upon awakening interior sensate abilities. Soon enough, it feels like I am drawing a powerful flow of energy up through my roots, legs, lower pelvis, and lower belly, into the solar plexus area.

My diaphragm seeks rich inhalations and exhaustive exhalations, as if hiking in mountains above accustomed altitudes. Eternal emptiness—eternal fullness extends into the space between breaths, like a comfortable silence between familiar friends. Attention focuses like hungry eyes on the subtle inner sensation of sinuous energy moving and flowing. An electrical-like charge of energy almost itches in my spine. Attending to the stillness between breaths increases the internal sensitivity to the sensation of energy stirring, responding to intention.

My mind tries to insert itself into the experience. It wants to interpret, if not understand.

Shut down your mind, Larry. I keep reminding myself. *Just let yourself have the experience. Explore the subtle inner sensations— that you feel, like warm water trickling over the skin, inside. There is a whole world in here. Allow yourself the purity of experience. Shut down your mind. Be in the memory of the caress of breasts, nipples inviting attention, and this mysterious territory of landscape lying at the apex of legs and groins joining. The stamina of women for lovemaking, for one orgasm after another, sometimes exceeding my own masculine capacity for meeting. Their hunger is easily equal to or even exceeds mine.*

Is a fear of these feminine desires and powers the originating seed of the masculine suppression of women? Jealous, are we? Jealous of their sexual capacity or of the mystery of their life creation powers? So many questions!

Soon it really is as if there is a serpent-like energy rising up my spine. With each slow deliberate inhalation, I draw it a little stronger and higher up. While it slightly sinks with the exhalations, like water coming up the pipe of an old-time hand pump, each inhalation of energy brings the force, the rising serpent's slither, to a higher level than previously.

Pull it up, more, stronger, yes. Let it sink. Again, pull it up with this breath in, more, deeper... till my heart also, like the areas below, feels open, full, and warm, charged with intensity. Love for the world fills me, for life, my life, until I feel my heart is not big enough to contain this affection that flows into and spills from me.

Breathe, Larry. Keep building it. Open. Pull it up. Let yourself be this energy. I remember my sensation on the cliff of being breathed. It is as if there is some subtle internal shift in which I become breath itself, as if breath is breathing me.

I search inside for the experience of this incredible place of shifting, as if it is a location on a map while holding also to the intention of pulling energy up into my throat area, the fifth chakra. I feel a congestion here, more so than in any of the previous areas. I must work harder to gain the sensation of energy flowing upward from my throat. But it does.

I continue pulling energy upwards until it rises into my forehead, the third eye, I've heard it called. It is as if, indeed, there is another organ of sensation and perception here, right in the center of my forehead. Its presence so distinct I feel I can almost wink it!

I do not want to imagine something not actually there, so with my eyes closed, I try to open all my internal senses yet further.

I find if I just bring the air deep into my pelvis first, and then let the energy build, the energy begins to make its way up naturally, migrating like a rising snake into the lower belly. With each breath, I can draw a little more energy in, build it to fullness, then draw it as if by suction further up the spine, into my heart—wounded, scared, and opening. It continues up into the throat, and the forehead, before spilling out the top of my head like water from a geyser, connecting me with the stars.

With pleasure and surprise, I begin drawing energy simultaneously from the outer reaches of the cosmos down through the top of my head, my spine, and into the earth. Soon inhalations spew energy out into space, and exhalations release the energy of the cosmos down, down deeper and deeper, as my roots grow toward the center of Earth herself.

I am the Tree of Life. Rooted. Branching and foliated. It lives within me.

I let go of everything but the moment's experience, then surrendered to the cosmos, and feel energy from its furthest reaches flow down through my head and body, out the soles of my feet, and on down through my roots. *I am a conscious energy lung of the universe, being breathed.*

Throughout all this my hands play with the leather, almost unconsciously, to see what might emerge. Parallel folds appear, something like the labia of a woman. *Yes! I like that. A vulva out of leather, Larry. Your own personal one, since you can't seem to keep any others around.* I laugh at myself and try to dive deeper. *But what is this essence of woman—of the feminine? Breathe in, Larry. Bring the energy up your roots and out—hold on to it nowhere—just let it move through you. Feel the silence of the place in between breaths. Be the fullness and let it release like the inevitable flow of water down a river. Let go into the emptiness, Larry.*

What if I make a nipple between the folds of leather? Yes, that's good, Larry. But there is something missing. Keep working it. I am in labor and then I see the emerging nipple under my fingers is also becoming an eye. *Yes! A way of perceiving. There's something here about the feminine capacity for orgastic ecstasy, and a mother's/*

lover's eros of life... that culture suppresses? Something about a way of seeing and being...?

And with this, my body quivers with the electrical power flowing through me. I am a white light shooting through this body. I am light. I am in a state of continuous cosmic whole-body orgasm. Surges of pleasure run up and down my spine and wash through my body. It is ecstasy without a bodily center, and it lasts a long, long time (Moali 2023).

Even after the intense somatic electricity charges settle down, even after the trembling eases, I am a light-being with roots that reach down into the core of the earth. A beam of light out the top of my head reaches into the cosmos. I am pure conscious energy. One with all there is.

I continue playing the leather with my fingers, pulling, stretching, folding to get the shapes right, refining the pupil of the eye itself into a distinct nipple, cradled by the labia of the vulva.

Later, I make the sculpture into a totem shield of sorts. The folds of the labia spread open to the eye with its pupil-nipple in the center. This is attached to a circle of soft elk hide sewn onto a circular frame. Four found wild turkey feathers, signifying energies such as connectivity, gratitude, a love of Nature and her abundance, the courage to be myself, and the honoring of community, hang by leather strips and grace the sides.

It is interesting to observe and confess from this distance of nearly fifty years later that I write that the sculpture lacks a distinct clit, a clitoris apart from the pupil/nipple. I was yet too wrapped in sexual shame during this era to study and explore female anatomy and pleasure consciously. I didn't know how to talk about sex and pleasure with my partners.

And even with *liberated women* of the time, sex was mostly just something we did. The forbidden territories of my fundamentalist world, still alive within, certainly did not include such freedoms of explorations. The personal, religious, cultural, and political implications run deep and far. It's also interesting to note that the culturally groundbreaking book, *The Joy of Sex,* published in 1972 and written by a man, did not mention the clitoris (Comfort 1972).

Is it any wonder I knew no one to share such an ecstatic, altered state experience with? *Who can advise me on the nature of such realities? Clearly, I lack some reliable orienting references to the true nature of my Self, and so too of what it is to truly be human.*

But am I crazy? Mad? Can sexual energy, life energy, and spiritual energy all be the same? Or have I only stumbled into some weird but privately ecstatic experience? Are there really chakras, vortices of spiritual anatomy, unseen by Western science that somehow reflect an individual's spiritual development? Might the chakras represent a system of insight into the evolutionary development of human consciousness?

And what of this entwining masculine and feminine energy? And given that we are innately wired for ecstatic potentialities, why is such knowledge forbidden? Who benefits? And what or who might I become if I live true to and trust myself?

These are wild and crazy questions!

When I now share such with my friend, Mark, who also knows what it is to walk the cultural edge of madness, he replies with a saying of which I am fond.

"The human experiment is littered with the bones of those
who chose to trust someone else's experience
instead of their own."

Carl Jung and Joseph Campbell grow as resources of investigation into this deep inner-self and world I am exploring. When I read of Carl Jung asking himself what the organizing myths of his life are, I, of course, ask the same of myself.

When I read Carl Jung's writings on the importance of the sacred marriage of one's inner masculine and feminine, or the importance of facing and integrating one's own inner shadows, to become a "whole person," I sense a North Star of commitment to my own journey of individuation.

I also recognize how out of touch with this body I am too. How constricted and emotionally shut down I am, how the emotional residue of my childhood lives in my armored body and restricts my access to love and joy. How it challenges my ability to "follow your bliss," as Campbell would say of the Hero's path in life. Explorations into the somatic therapy work of Wilhelm Reich, Alexander Lowen, and Ida Rolf lead me to attend the College of Natural Medicine in Santa Fe, NM, now defunct, during my off-fire season. I'm also drawn to the school because I want to study life as expressions of pure energy, vibration, and frequency. And this school offers training in Energy Healing and Polarity Therapy.

I just know there is so much I do not know, so little wattage in the light of my knowledge. And this hunger to know the truth of life drives my search for understanding, meaning, and purpose in life. Fortunately, on some level, I do recognize my willingness to *not know* is a strength, for one who is lost, anyway. This awareness of my ignorance comes with personal and social vulnerabilities, however. Yet it adds the gift of a keen edge to my explorations of life—the willingness to engage as a learner.

One in Love with Forest Folks

Carelessly I spooked them
startled them into running
maybe thirty yards before stopping
turning in curiosity to see
or smell if possible who or what
walked in among them so unannounced
as to almost be one of them.

But no, he's a two-legged one
moving slowly and singing something
a lover's melody about awe and beauty
dark doe eyes and tan fur and long ears
slender legs of grace and lips for choosing
and a white rump as tails lift in flight...

I shall dress more carefully next time
being sure to wear my antlers
and wrap in my tan blanket of fur
remembering to walk alertly
as I sniff the air for odors
left by the women kind for such as I
one in love with forest folks
whether they be wearers of fur or bark
scales or feathers or fins matters not
for I am no discriminator
against this deep self of origin and nourishment
my family of my belonging.

Chapter 10

THE MEDICINES OF CONNECTION

Learning to walk in multiple worlds of differing dimensions comes more graciously and consciously to me through time, by stumble and trip, fortune, desire, and hunger to know more of who I am and how it is our world operates. It takes decades for me to notice that I am following a game trail of synchronicities.

This learning to track my own spirit's journey through life is akin to learning to see and follow, for the exploratory joy of it, the faint trails of forest critters, whether bear, deer, elk, squirrels, or yet smaller mysteries. The more I attune myself to noticing the *odd alignments* amidst my living, the more they seem to occur. It's like dreaming of someone and running into them the next day. Or like realizing one wants to learn about some idea and then spontaneously opening a book off the shelf to a page, exploring the idea.

Soon enough, one takes notice not only of the sharp-pointed hoof print of, say, a deer, and then you find yourself using sticks to pull apart the trail scatt to see who's been eating whom. Then you find yourself on your knees or belly eyeing and wondering about the patterned paths or signatures of ants and mice and more.

I find myself living not so much in a Cartesian world of objects as in a holographic world woven of dimensional relationships. This learning to read the energetic signatures within an ecological system serves me well as it leaves my self-identity less attached to beliefs for a sense of solidity to my being. A paradoxical increased sense of security and belonging gift me with more availability for the transformations of heart, body, and mind I feel the world asking of me. And indeed, my own metamorphosis out of the righteous world of good against evil will require my spirit to remember how to fly.

Who, for example, might have predicted the role pedophile Catholic priests might play in this personal transformation?

Other than paganism, the deceived worshipers of nature with their evil witches and illusionary earth spirits, Catholicism was Satan's next most wicked institution—them and the Muslims we were still in a Holy War against. And of course, the Lutherans, Methodists, and Southern Baptists, and I'm going to pull myself out of this rabbit hole of hierarchically naming all the evils out there as I learned them.

Back to the Catholic Church, however. My view of that institution, as *the spawn of the Devil*, had not improved since my own becoming an outcast of the church of my rearing. Then came one of those phone calls that changed my life.

I was still at the Mountain Center, along about 1984, and had moved from field staff to Logistical Director to Clinical Director, when Rocky got the call from a psychiatrist working at the Servants of the Paraclete in Jemez Springs, NM.

"Let's go over and see what they're interested in," he says.

We end up providing five-day therapeutic wilderness programs, twice a year, for three groups of eight men in each, for about four years. The programs consist of backpacking, a twenty-four-hour solo experience, and a day of rock-climbing and rappelling. We then provide written and verbal assessments of each participant back to the staff at the local treatment facility. (I come to consider it essentially a 'closet facility' for what will, not soon enough, blow up into a huge problem for the church.)

Anthony is a rotund and short man with a Brooklyn accent on one of these programs with me. His offense includes the known sexual abuse of over one hundred young men, which is, unfortunately, not as unusual as it should be. We are camped at the bottom of a canyon of astounding volcanic origins and beauty in the Jemez Mountains. Old-growth ponderosa pines and Douglas firs tower and spiral upwards around us and root deeply into ancient rocky soil. A rare trickling Southwestern seventy-foot waterfall is just down canyon, slightly off to the side of the one-hundred-foot rappel site. The slit of New Mexico's blue sky runs north and south overhead.

Anthony, along with his peers, is freshly back into base camp off his solo. We stand on the pine-needle-covered forest floor and the air smells of treasures like a privilege too few will ever know. He is but two or three feet in front of me, and I feel a confrontation coming as his eyes stare into mine.

"You look out here and see beauty," he says. "I look out here and all I see is death."

It is a simple and informative statement from this man of God. And it is a hit to my solar plexus. I have no response, for I, too, see what he sees.

We *are* indeed surrounded by death. Dead pine needles crunch under our feet. Dead trees tower above us as other trunks litter the forest floor, accumulating from our one-hundred-year-old cultural holy war against *evil* forest fires. The gathering of dead wood for our campfire tonight will come easily. Yes, I see, too, that we are surrounded by death. But I also see what he does not.

I see Death is held within the sacred circle, a cycle of life, death, and rebirth. The Ouroboros, the ancient image of a snake or dragon, eating its tail, illustrates death feeding life and life feeding death as polarities existing within the Tree of Life. Anthony sees the world through the lens of the Tree of Knowledge, through the dualities of Life versus Death, and the war of Good against Evil.

But with Anthony's declaration, I now emotionally swim in centuries of religious dogma, a story of humankind's separation from our very belonging to the Tree of Life itself. As if such a thing were even possible!

I swim in the theologies of suppression, subjugation, superiority, and domination that leave men themselves victims of a puritanical God of perpetration—one who declares the gift of bodily-sensuality as dangerous and not to be trusted. I imagine centuries of such spiritual abuse ritually and shamefully passed down from Father to altar boy acolyte. I see the Stockholm Syndrome, wherein the abused identify with and ultimately imitate their abuser. I see an entire Western Culture bowing in unconscious subservience to the perpetuation of a loss of reference from our innate divine nature. From Nature, Earth herself, as reference for the forbidden divine feminine within. Thus, the divine masculine is also forbidden intimacy with itself, and we are left with fragmented, wounded, and toxic ideologies of what it is to *be a man*.

And so, the sins of God, and of the Father, are indeed visited upon the sons and daughters for generations to come.

With time, I come to see Anthony's gifts to me. He helps me see that much of my work in the world has been simply to "help people learn to see their face in the forest," as I like to say. *I yearn to help folks see that the beauty they see in a sunset or magnificent tree or in the fluttering butterfly is but one of their own faces.*

Anthony also highlights for me a vital principle that, within these yearnings for belonging and worthiness, time in nature by itself is not what can gift us with healing and transformation. No! It is the quality of presence we bring to the encounter that makes the difference: whether it be with the eyes of Spirit and an open heart that perceives or feels the inherent mystery and wonder within another, or the encultured eye and heart that see and feel the world commodified, objectified, and so fallen and devoid of inherent divinity and sovereignty.

Anthony and his cohorts place also another gift on my altar-of-life. He invites me to witness the victim hiding within the perpetrator. Yes! He invites me to open my heart to empathy and compassion for myself and all others caught in unconscious theological worldviews of victimization from a so-called "all-powerful loving god" of conditional love, and who so must eternally seek outside ourselves for love and worthiness. What loneliness!

It is a beautiful gift of synchronicity that, upon leaving the Mountain Center in 1988, I follow Rocky's professional lead into experiential organizational learning and development. With this comes about seven years of paid opportunities for study and practice in the fields of creativity, leadership, and high performance, of emotional literacy and intelligence, of skills for accessing collective intelligence and wisdom, and more intensified inquiries into the development of human consciousness and transformation.

Synchronistically, upon leaving the Mountain Center, I am gifted with the opportunity to provide programs to the Sangre de Cristo Retreat Center, a non-therapeutic Christian Brothers program. For roughly the next eight years I host the same essential program once provided for the pedophile priests, but now for each of Sangre's twice-annual one-hundred-day renewal programs.

And what a delight and honor it is to be of service to the priests, brothers, and nuns from something like thirty nations. They are people of the heart seeking to serve their God through serving the "least among us." They are beautiful soulful spirits in human form, inspired by eyes open to wonder and awe. They are hungry and grateful for the self-renewal that arrives as they learn to see "their face in the forest."

And when, in preparation for their twenty-four-hour wilderness solos, I teach "how to take a dump in the woods," their worlds turn as I begin the instructions. "This is an invitation to feed your shit consciously back to the Mother." Their mouths drop open, but I continue.

"Consider that the food generating the waste you are about to bury comes from the same soil, water, air, and sun that your wondrous fleshy bags of a body do. I invite you to consider your taking a dump out here as a sacred, conscious gifting back, with gratitude to Earth, for feeding you in the first place and for then composting your waste into the making of new soil. This fertile forest soil is richer in DNA density than is the DNA density of your brain." I pause before continuing to let this sink in.

"Yeah, this is living earth. LIVING dirt, if you will, and all the little critters, bacteria, fungi, and such together make for a kind of intelligent community within which everything is endlessly recycled. Apart from human systems, there is no 'waste' in nature."

"And within a cubic inch of this soil, there might be more than eight miles of mycelium cells, collectively weaving the forest floor and all the trees and shrubs and flowers and grasses around us into a symbiotic community. These little individual white hair-like threads you see here, under this rock I've turned over, are called mycelia. Mushrooms, it turns out, are the fruiting body, the reproductive spore-producing sexual organs, if you will, of the larger fungal-mycelium bodies of which there are yet many unidentified species."

"Some mycologists think of mycelium as a neurological network of nature. They are akin to both the neural cells of our brains, literally transferring information between various plants, and to our blood vessels too because they also actively transfer nutrients throughout the forest system."

"Now we're gonna talk about digging a hole, location, depth, and all that in a moment. But first, I invite you to consider also what other shit, waste, or baggage you carry through life that you might let go of and *give back to the Mother*, or to Spirit or God...during your time here. What shames or guilts, what regrets or sorrows might you desire to compost, to make fertile and beautiful soil of?"

"And what gratitudes might you offer, as long as we're at this? And what might our world become if we learn to see through the eyes of Nature's principle of *reciprocity wherein giving and receiving are inextricably entwined*? What if the giver is also the receiver, and the receiver is also the one gifting?"

Oh, but I am a blessed man! Not just for playing the role of provocateur here. But also for experiencing the essential and elemental commonality within this diversity of clientele. What a gift to experience our common humanity—from victimized abuse survivors to juvenile delinquents, robbers, rapists, murderers, government and corporate executives, therapists, pedophile priests, and saints offering their lives for the well-being of those with only gratitude to give in return. What a privilege to have intimately worked with them all! To see their face in mine and my face in theirs!

And what a gift to experience minds projecting upon the world, through the lens of our inner eye, the very vision constructed by the story of our worldview. It's like the often-cited yet source-unknown phrase: "We do not see things as they are, we see them as we are."

The world is a mirror. Every thought reflects to us the divine, creative powers of our own souls. And to learn to walk and be upon the land with the practices and powers of such inner awareness is to become again indigenous to Earth. It is soma and spirit entwining in the knowledge that we belong to her and are of her.

It is to reside in the experience of living as beings born of the stars and of unknowns of yet greater magnitude, while washing diapers and navigating rush hour traffic on your way to the airport... And it is in the self-interest of our capitalistic global economy and structures of social power to distract us from discovering and owning this very discovery and perception.

I am sitting with friends at a local café when a woman of roughly my age unexpectedly approaches. "Are you Larry Glover?"

"Uh, yes," I fess up, not quite sure what might follow. I've led wilderness and non-wilderness programs with thousands of folks by now, so I cannot begin to remember all those who have reciprocally touched my heart. Yet her appearance does have me thinking she looks familiar. And it is a relatively small town I live in so...

"Well," she continues, "I had a dream about you. I wasn't sure who you were, but I recognized you. I had to ask my son, Sam. You worked with him years ago. And you and I met in my driveway once. Yeah. In the dream, you told me I need to get out into nature and to spend more time with the trees."

A healthy and pleasurable laugh escapes me. I've often been told by program participants, sometimes years later, that when they notice a particularly striking tree, they think of me. I am learning that self-love means no longer needing to run from or chase the love of others.

And I also have an old pattern of attempting not to allow in too deeply what folks think of me. It's a habit of self-protection, given my dual-edged hunger for attention and love, my early hypersensitivity to and the subsequent need to distance and protect myself from the criticisms of church folks, and my early developed determination to *be my own man* and to *go against the grain*—my cultivated *lone cowboy* self-image.

A clear shadow side of these patterns, however, is the spiraling challenge of allowing in other people's love or esteem of me. *Obviously, I hunger for everyone to love me! And fear the same!*

But to go more intimately deeper, just the spiral of learning to love myself—to really bring *L O V E* to this self, no exceptions—continues. I am reminded of the locally common petroglyphs of spirals carved into many a boulder or cliff face by Puebloan Native Americans. Including the marking of seasonal solstices or equinoxes, some of these rock carvings are also said to represent physical or spiritual migrations.

My precious and inspiring friend, Jaquelina Barra, founder of Ama Tu Luna (amatuluna.com) and part of the Cosmic Community, through which she "works for the well-being of the planet by promoting paths of sustainability for human health and all living beings," recently opened afresh my own spiraling pilgrimage into love.

"Larry," she says with open frankness, "you're never going to finish your book or your life's work if you don't learn to love yourself. I saw this hole in your heart when we first met. You need to let Larry love Larry."

Damn! I can't believe she just said this to me. I've never held myself with as much self-love as now! Crap! And this, too, during an era and summer when I have felt bathed in love and appreciation by friends and program participants, literally. Like the four-day program Cheryl and I just hosted a few weeks back, Heart Practices in Nature: a Hiking and Meditation Retreat, ended with so much love coming my way.

Jaqui's right, though. I see it as I get quiet and honest with myself now. I do have a hard time letting love into the hidden recesses of my heart. I say, "Thank you," but then don't really let it in. I'm afraid to. I am afraid of love! Of its power. Of the transformations it invites me into.

Yeah, my heart does have a hole in it. It's scary to really let in how much people love me. I need to learn to bring love-of-self home!

Hell, I'm still trying to figure out what to do with one participant's love when they said in our closing debrief, with total affection and respect, "I want Larry to be my Spirit Animal!"

I share this personally heart-touching reflection here because it provokes my vulnerability. No, Mom and Dad, and God, this is not about bragging. It is to claim more fully and step into the essence of what this book represents for me. It is to celebrate the transformative gifts this spiritual resonance with Nature, this love of the wild bestows on my living. And it is to be a finger pointing to the uncountable galaxies and stars we swim amidst, to point to Moon and the cycling phases of her death and rebirth, if you will, and to say, *"I am but a pilgrim here too. And we are all so much more wondrous than my evangelical upbringing led me to believe. And this bringing of love home to Self is the greatest challenge the Jehovah-wound leaves one with."*

I also seek with this sharing to invite the inquiry: What might it be like if we look to each other, and to the trees or creatures or elements that call out for our attention, as Spirit Animals or Sacred Totems, as sacred mirrors or allies? For indeed, the entire cosmos is talking to us, inviting us to listen.

It is love that invites me to begin a deeper listening into the Quaking Aspen (Populus tremuloides). There's an aspen grove in south-central Utah, named Pando (I spread). It comprises some estimated 47,000 individual-looking trees spread over 106 acres.

But the truth is, what looks to be a captivating forest of tall white single-stemmed trees here, some up to eighty feet tall and 150 years old, is a single organism. To walk within Pando, or any aspen grove, is to walk inside the communal and symbiotic body of an organism.

The trees here carry identical genetic markers as they share a single massive interconnecting root system from which each *tree* arises, as a clone, or ramet. This leaves Pando in a class of its own as to the largest trees, compared to, say, the giant sequoia, General Sherman in California, the largest, by volume, single-stemmed tree. Pando, however, is the world's heaviest known organism and largest tree by landmass.

I have long talked with all I encounter that is wild—the animals, soil, trees, water, fire, wind, the directions, and the stars and moon. But there is something about aspens that keeps drawing the attention and curiosities of my soul and spirit. The more I spend time in their presence, the more I research them, the more enchanted I become.

Take their relationship with fire, for example. They are historically often the first tree to *recolonize* an area after large-scale fire events in the Rocky Mountains. They are sun-loving and a fire that might take out shade-loving spruces, for example, opens the area for a decades- or centuries-long *hibernating* root system to awaken and express above ground again as an aspen grove.

In addition to aspens being among Earth's largest organisms, they are among the oldest living ones. Pando has been dated to at least 16,000 years old and may be as old as 81,000 years, making it one of the most ancient of living beings. And the truth is, we do not know how old they may live to be.

Aspens evolved in northern climates with cold winters, and the white bark is another developmental adaptation. The white acts as a protective sunscreen for the tree, and after rubbing your hands onto the trunk, you can rub the resulting chalky white powder onto your face for sunscreen. And should you ever so carefully, and with the tree's permission, cut into the thin layer of white skin, immediately below is a green layer filled with chlorophyll. This evolutionary development allows the tree to conduct photosynthesis during the long winters of its evolutionary development.

It is a full moon mountain winter night when I know the time is right for me to drop into a mushroom medicine journey with Aspen. Sudden Aspen Decline (SAD) has hit the species particularly hard in the US with some western states losing up to 90% of their lower elevation stands, and I fear for those near my mountain cabin refuge. Climate change is, of course, a primary suspect among the causes even as it portends the end of the forested landscapes of today's familiarity.

I am not alone in my fear of the loss of forested landscapes, as I have been privileged to know them. Scientists now seek means to help trees migrate as our heating planet and climatic disruptions challenge and change the very environmental stabilities modern culture is dependent upon. My heart is having a hard time knowing how to meet this world of increasing tensions and accelerating change. I need help in seeing both myself and the world differently, and so I turn to this old ally of the sacred fungus, as humans have since the earliest of our times. I seek help in attuning myself to the world as it is, even as I seek to touch and re-anchor to the deep Self of my own being.

Ritual incorporation of deep, somatic, conscious breathing and movement in the early and later portions of my medicine journeys is invaluable to their embodiment and integration for me. Slow, mindful hiking through the forest simply with time spent in the presence of the wild is ideal. On this winter night, I seek to spend time with the aspens before my desired arrival back at the cabin, before the full onset of the medicine's booster second ingestion leaves me capable only of lying on the floor, riding the inner waves of communion with the cosmos.

Meanwhile, I hang out in a nearby grove and attune my system to its vibrational frequency. I feel the sensuous serpentine rooting below and the rising slender white trunks rising above. I sit and walk within the aspen body. "Let me see your true face," I pray as a mantra, even as their white-barked trunks shimmer on the moonlit side and are shadowed on the opposite.

I am drawn to an elder I often sit with and walk to it, my entheogenic-holographic vision incorporating the wonder and truth of being with this one in full presence is to be with the whole of the grove.

I anticipate the wild joy of touching this beautiful being with the heart's reach of my right hand, to enjoy the pleasure of touching each and all of them—for they are what I come to call The One Rooted One. Before reaching out, however, my eyes are drawn to look up the length of the trunk and its branching into the starry sky and then follow its straight trunk downward to where it enters the field of snow.

My active imagination is now peering holographically into the depths of the two-foot snowbank gathered around the tree. It is as if the light of colors in the sparkling stars overhead now twinkles like diamonds from within the snow itself. But there, coiled, awake, and present to my presence, is a large white serpent with two black eyes.

I am stunned beyond any ability to believe in what I am seeing—still cognizant enough to know I am hallucinating. I fall to my knees in awe and wonder at the beauty and mystery, the potency and vitality of life force that is perceived by the entirety of my being as a weaving together of the totality of the forest—symbolized in my system as a coiled aspen-white serpent whose black eyes meet my gaze and pierce my soul. Time stops.

I notice my breath has unconsciously paused as Bear again arrives and reminds me to begin, and so begin conscious, deep, rhythmic breaths, touching the stillness between inhalation and exhalation. I maintain conscious embodiment as my system begins to allow in this experience that is beyond all imagination and description—the unreality of it, and the deeper reality that I am in witness to, and partaker and co-creator of.

Even as my system wants to ask, who are you, I realize, "You're the naked Life Force of Aspen looking at me, and I at you, all dressed up to suit my story and psyche, too." I sense the snake-like roots as they coil and wind their way through the mountain's soil. I remember Serpent as a consort of the goddess of old, the One, the feminine power Jehovah was jealous of and so forbade the worship of. I experience the cosmos as pervasive sentient consciousness itself, a oneness mirrored within the one rooting of Aspen, and I experience Love as the weaver that all the cosmos and life are rooted into and from.

Yes! Life is, of course, in love with itself! That's why it is self-sustaining and self-renewing! It is always coming home to itself—through the myriad forms of diversity's expressions. How else could Oneness know and experience itself except through this cyclic interplay of polarities and individuations, of forgetting and of re-membering?

I sense the eros of Life's and Spirit's love-of-embodiment, of incarnation as inhalation—and exhalation as the release back into the womb of the Great Mother. *I partake of this cycle of life—with every breath!*

Oh, hello! Here you are again, you madness of my youth. I see you: you, the madness that nearly killed me many a time. You, the madness that drove me to the Lookout! You, the madness that needs heroic and grandiose specialness. "Oh, yeah, Larry. You are the One *returning again and again throughout the ages in multitudes of expression. The Christ Returned!"*

This is not personal, I tell and assure myself. It is not about Larry, but it *is the recognition of a sacred seed living in everyone. Just waiting to wake up. This is not about me being The One—being someone special.*

No. It is rather a deep leveling of water returning to source, wherein all is an expression of Source.

My vision deepens into a spiritual and somatic witness to the flow of spirals-of-awakening running through the course of my life. I recognize this itch for awakening back in my high school speech, *The Man Nobody Knows*. This expression within Christian mystical traditions is referenced as Christ Consciousness, or *The Universal Christ*, as Franciscan friar Richard Rohr writes of it (Rohr 2019). Two of but many names the unspeakable mystery wears through the dimensions of time and space.

I too am woven of and from love. I am love—in the essence of my deepest self.

This is what the Biblical Christ figure knew and shared. No separation or mediation between self and the divine is needed, but love itself. For the unspeakable mystery is Love. Innate love, belonging, worthiness, and kinship with all of life—these are the forbidden fruits of the Tree of Life, that no human mother would consciously deny her children.

I partake fully of these fruits as aspens reveal themselves to me as Spirit and Soul Medicine for our times, as an ecologically imaginative and embodied metaphor of the Tree of Life. And the Serpent, the skin-shedding Serpent, is consort to the goddess.

"I welcome you, Serpent. I welcome you." I repeat this as a mantra as I feel Serpent's awakening within, representative of Life's powers of death and rebirth and eternal life throughout time—fruits of the Tree of Life, Serpent shedding its skin, time and again.

I welcome this conscious partaking of the forbidden fruit, the fruit from "the other tree" in the mythical and Biblical Garden of Eden. I've stumbled my way past the Guardians at the Gate. Serpent is alive and present and moving within me, awakening and enlivening my spine and within all that is. There is no separation. All is divine.

My consciousness is now one with Aspen too. One with Forest and River and Stars. One with Earth as the womb of Life as I know it. There is no explanation or naming for such an identity, except one of three thousand years of antiquity: I Am That I Am.

And, I am, that we are. We are, that I am too.

Oh, but this is madness! I dance at the edges of madness. Yet I can imagine nothing truer than what I am experiencing. I do not know how to carry this in the world, how to share such gifting, but to cultivate space consciously for the radiance of Love the best I can.

And I feel Serpent's wisdom speak, "Release, shed even this desire. And shed too the fear of not being enough to Love."

I stumble my way back to the cabin, lay on the yoga mat in front of the blazing fireplace, and invite Serpent deeper into my body. I attend to breath and allow my body to move spontaneously with the impulses of awakening within. Eventually, I put on music and dance into embodiment and celebration, this embrace with the goddess, and her honored companion, Serpent. I dance a celebration of the masculine, invite in the feminine, my Sophia. *My dear love, Gaia, Mother, Help Me Know How To Carry This!*

For the following two years, I see serpents everywhere. Snakes spontaneously appear in my vision and crawl around, on and inside, the walls at home and in restaurants. I see Serpent inside people as I walk the grocery store aisles. Serpent winds and coils up, and down, and within trees. Boulders are slithering Serpent nests in bone. Soil is alive with the vital energy of hundreds and thousands of dimensionally intermingling snakes. They feel my footsteps as I walk gently within Forest and offer gratitude and blessings. Trees notice my passing—with or without my acknowledgment—and Serpent looks back at me in the mirror, eye to eye.

Who can I tell? How can I tell?

What is this Aspen and Serpent lover to do? Celebration requires I continue to offer and refine various wilderness and nature-based programs, but now with the ecology of aspens as core to their themes. Themes like:

- Aspens—Ancient Wisdom for Thriving in a Turbulent World
- Inquiries into an Ecology of Care: Taking Care of Self-Care
- Loneliness and Presence: What the Aspen Know
- Forbidden Knowledge and the Aspen
- Wilderness Skills Intensive: Nurturing Renewal and Resilience through Your Love of Nature
- Wilderness Skills Intensive for Loving Self and Life
- Journey into Creativity—Inspired and Informed by Nature
- Decline, Collapse, and Rebirth: Lessons from Nature for Wholehearted Living in Today's World
- Wild Resiliency: Coming Home to Yourself
- How to be Lost—and Found: Practical Mind, Body, Heart and Wilderness Skills for Navigating Uncertain Terrain and Times

I do not, however, so publicly share this story of the Snow Serpent until now. Perhaps it is this counsel from the Gospel of Thomas that moves my sharing:

If you give birth to what's within you, what you have within you will save you. If you do not have that within [you], what you don't have within you [will] kill you.

—Gospel of Thomas (Verse 70)

—Mark M Mattison

The Gospel of Thomas: A Public Domain Translation

Or maybe this share is an active surrender to "the madness" at last. And to its redemption. For how could this personal dissonance be any worse than the insanity of separation now coming to a crescendo in our divisive political, religious, and cultural spheres? Memories of diverse clientele and programs flash through my system.

I remember the hundreds of spiritually wounded and angry or depressed young men I've led into the wilds of Nature. Mad, they all were—mad for belonging, meaning, and love.

And I wonder where our children will find purpose and meaning as they swim in a world where the infectious wounds of separation and suppression, the Jehovah wound itself, are not recognized as a spiritual trauma.

I remember hosting a twenty-four-hour Wilderness Solo event for fifty international senior business executives. How might this spiritual madness and trauma of disconnection play out in the leadership of those who have never slept on naked Earth alone through the night, befriended the wilds within and the wilds without as intimate companions?

I feel the body, sexual shame, and madness of abuse, propagated, hidden, and covered up by prominent religious, civic, and political organizations, in self-interest though under the banner of God and Country.

I am torn into sorrow and grief by the madness of strategies of war on a planet too small for more.

I wonder how dead to themselves do people have to become before their wounded souls say, "Enough!" Before they recognize complicity and rebel against a cultural story embracing suicide through cannibalism of Mother Earth? Must they first become seduced by mad men presenting themselves as God's chosen political or religious saviors?

Perhaps this madness of our times is more interestingly seen as an escalating invitation into remembering that this forbidden shared divinity, already living within, is foundational to viable paths into our future. The wound of the original heresy is a shared one, and together we awaken from it.

And then I remember the quote from Joseph Campbell: "In choosing your god, you choose your way of looking at the universe." (Campbell 1991, 163)

And then other connective threads of consciousness return... like the beauty, the wild joys of walking with naked feet touching bare soil. I remember sitting in presence with the wholeness of Aspen, and I breathe in the rebirth of a Self. And with my exhale, I offer back this life in service to the mystery and wholeness of who we each are.

I need such practices, rituals, ceremonies, community, and solitude to support my joyful living amidst a world gone mad with the normalization of separation. This requires daily breathing in the divine, deep cosmological self that life reveals me to be. The seductions into sleepwalking grow stronger with technology's indiscriminate aid in service of economic and political agendas. These practices nurture the container, the self, that navigates my daily world and attracts nurturance and natural abundance while also, best able, setting boundaries on the predators and parasites and toxicities of our human landscapes too.

I Go to the Mountains to Pray

from within the rooted
oneness of Aspen's body
and from the temple where singing waters emerge

Here water gurgles and springs out beneath a granite bolder
protector of the Mother's womb-of-darkness below
while but yards away two creeks join as one
amplify the sacred medicine of this holy incarnation

Where the entire world can be touched
felt and held in the One Heart
that honors diversity and differentiation
yet knows no separation

Here I drink from the Waters of Life
lay offerings of gratitude
and beseech of Forest
Teach me

For I yearn to learn better
to perceive the mycelium thread
of the One Root of Love
weaving the world into Wholeness

Upon uttering this prayer
a gentle breeze kisses my cheek and makes visible
weavings of light glistening in play with shadows
to reveal Spider's intricate shimmering web

My heart opens as awe and love converge and overflow
as she comes forth to speak

Says
      Be Still
          Listen
               with the innate belonging
                     of your original body

for your life and prayers depend
upon your willingness

to sing your self
and the World anew into being
rooted into the Tree of Life
as One

Chapter 11

CAIRNS OF THE HEART

I received a diagnosis predicting six to eight months to live, roughly five months ago as I write this. "You have an incurable and terminal Stage 4 non-small cell lung cancer. It has metastasized to the left hip and femur."

My world flips upside down as these words reverberate through my body. This afternoon's weather forecast is not the one of this morning. Tomorrow's, and the month's calendar, are erased to make room for ever-growing numbers of lab tests and doctor visits. My life is aswirl with unknowns, especially when the oncologist says, "No more hiking. Your bones are too fragile."

My heart breaks into uncontrollable sobbing. I wonder if such a life can be worth living, one without my soles kissing wild soils and me nestling in among the roots of Grandmother Spruce and conversing with the yet wild waters of the Pecos River.

Yet it is good news to at last gain an understanding of the causes behind increasing pains in my hip and a growing shortness of breath, night sweats, physical exhaustion, and other mysterious symptoms.

It is even better news later, though still confusing, when after DNA testing of the tumor, the oncologist announces, "You've won the lottery, Larry! The genetic testing reveals you have a cancer rarely found in men! And there's an experimental daily oral chemo you can take that is designed to target this specific cancer that can greatly improve your chances for a longer life. And we can increase your chances further with the use of radiation and IV chemo regimens."

The overall news, however, has been hard to incorporate, and the experience is challenging and yet unfolding. I share these intimacies not to recommend my path as *the way* but as an illustration of what it can be to meet the unsettled times of our living, say an *enemy story*, as a portal into self-revelation and deeper living, inspired and informed through intimacies with Nature.

I'm now, as I write this, three weeks out from my next PET scan, which will reveal if the *cancer* (not a word I like to use) is growing, temporarily stabilized, or continuing to shrink. Nature teaches me that a complete healing may be possible, but for now, I live in the unknown. And within this territory, I frankly have some anxiety as I await the upcoming test's revelations, as I was unable to complete the recommended every three-week two-drug IV chemotherapy cocktail regimen. My body screamed, "No More!" as I felt the treatments were taking me out beyond tolerance for my living. The quality of my living is more important to me than the length.

The questions arise, however, as I await the next test results: *Is the cancer actively taking me out? Or might I be at a stage of learning to live with the cancer, for some unknown time?* Once again, developed life strategies of coming to nature as a sacred teacher, healer, and lover inform my living and heighten my access to the life force itself. She teaches me to look at life through a lens of polarities rather than black-and-white dualities, of ecological perceiving and the science of living systems, of symbiotic connectivity, of relationally interwoven and interdependent energetics, of vibrations and frequencies being elemental and pervasive even at quantum levels (Sahtouris 2000).

This leads me to come to the *dis-ease* with eyes that recognize I and it are not separate. There is not, as I experience the circumstance, something outside of me attacking me. Rather, on the level of Spirit, since the cosmos (below the levels of manifest polarities) is woven of the mystery of love and Oneness in my experience, I look to gather the gifts that are here for me to claim and receive. This, even as I receive the best of Western and alternative medicines available, including from nature and the spirit world too. The impulse to boundary the reality of predators and parasites, including ideologies and theologies, that would consume our life energy for purposes of their own is an expression of self-love.

So, when I journeyed with the intention of meeting the "high-jacking hitchhiker," as I first came to reference it, I came to it in the spirit of self-love and with mantras of prayers. *"Let me see your true face... show me the essence of your energy... Why are you here? Who are you? What parts of me might you in some way reflect? What hidden gifts might you carry?"*

As I merge into the tumors with offerings of love, I feel the energetics of endless voraciousness, of unfillable hunger. *I sense within you no organizing principle or DNA of structure beyond consumption. You have no organizing purpose in life for integrating into the ecosystem of this body. You live for your boundless hunger, which will, in the end, terminate your life and mine. So, you are a servant of Death and Destruction, are you?*

Or might we together make some other, some life-affirming story and energy, some soul medicine—even if my Death is to arrive through you?

And as my mind is inclined to do, it quickly analogizes from the personal to the collective and back.

Oh, you're like capitalistic Western Culture, aren't you? Consumption and growth for their own sake, regardless of the health of the system you are embedded within (Catton 1982).

Simultaneously, I perceive, *You mirror the energetic signature of the Jehovah Wound I carry: there is never enough praise and love directed to that jealous God. He is always in need of more fleshly converts willing to sing his eternal praises in some Heaven, located in some mysterious out-there. Willing too, confessed "creator" of darkness and of evil that he is* (Isaiah 45:7), *to direct his jealous wrath against the men, women, and innocent babies of those who refuse to bow to him as the only one and true God, those who follow the goddess, and other images or conceptions of reality. And for the infected followers or true believers, there is never enough self-love that can be learned or received from a conditionally loving God.*

I sit, sense, and track this energy, to witness its playing out along the trails of my life. I recognize theological and habituated patterns of looking outside myself for approval and love, for a worthiness of life. I am yet breaking free of inseminated patterns of seeking domination, subjugation, and control over my own body, over my partners, over nature, and over life itself—as if such were even possible.

I look online for the etymology of the word *voracious* and find two that resonate. In the 1520s, the French began using the word *voracité* to refer to appetites of such greediness in living. I also like the proto-Indo-European root word, *gwora*, referring to "food, devouring."

I shall call you Gwora and Voracité, for I see you now. You're a version of the hitchhiker I met all those years back! Someone with a meta-story embedded with the need for an enemy out there to hate because they're unwilling to meet the enemy living within. Oh god, where and what enemies do I carry within that I am afraid to look at?

Judgments and victimization fall away as self-recognition spirals in yet deeper. This cancer is no more separate from me than is the water I drink daily of.

I bring you offerings of love and gratitude, dear Gwora, for I see you indeed also come with gifts. You carry invitations into greater awakening and gratitude for this life. You remind me to die before I die, *so I can live fully now! I am not separate from the cycle of life and death and rebirth. Thank you, oh my Death. Let me hold you as an adviser by my side until the time comes when we look into each other's eyes.*

And with this, I realize I am deep into a Death Lodge Journey, as I name the ten days and nights following my initial chemotherapy treatments. They create such indescribable depths of discomfort and a desire to just escape this fleshy bag of water for release. In these dark hours, I frequently cannot sleep. My body and system attempt to alchemize the lifesaving poisons injected into the flow of blood in my veins. But it is within this darkness of night that I discover gifts of insight beyond description. It is all I can do to breathe consciously, deeply, slowly, and exhaustively as initiated by Bear, reinforced on the cliff, and again when I picked up the lonely hitchhiker. The subsequent years of conscious breath practices once again enrich, if not save, my life, for I now find myself touching the metaphoric Tree of Life within, where Death abides too.

I rise from the root of this Tree of Life, and I begin to survive my nights by vitalizing this naked life force within as the sacred Breath of Life. I breathe in its life-affirming and gifting energy. And I release each breath with gratitude and actively surrender myself to Death with each exhalation. "Teach me to let go of what no longer serves," I pray with each out-breath. "Teach me to allow in and to be love, to pull in the innate healing powers of Nature," I pray, even as I breathe in these energetic vibrations. I lie in bed and become one with the mystery of Source.

Serpent is here with me too, in each breath. But not just one, not just White Serpent. No. Black Serpent is here now also, spontaneously arising imaginal manifestations of Shakti and Shiva. They dynamically entwine vertically around my spinal and chakra systems not as opposites but as polarities, wherein the two are one: birth and death, the feminine and masculine, the intermingling darkness of matter and the womb, and the light of sun and spirit, as a balance of being and doing, as chaos and order, destruction, and creation. Each granting and ensuring rebirth of the other in a great cycle of Life—surely a wonder and mystery beyond naming or understanding.

My Death Lodge is now also a womb. I am once again, through this intimacy with Death's continuous presence, with the entwining of destruction and creation, giving birth to a new self. And one morning, at about 2 a.m., I find myself singing a lullaby of love to Voracité, as part of who I am. *Go to sleep, my darlings, go to sleep... I bring you love and gratitude. And yes, I seek to boundary your presence. I invite you—please integrate into this body, in service of the larger whole, in service of a more beautiful story; if it may be so.*

And I honor you, for I feel your unbounded hunger for life. So please, teach me, I pray, how to live, and how to die. How to say "Yes!" to the two as One.

Sleepless hours at night, lying in bed and entering the altered states of physical and emotional exhaustion that accompany both the poisons of treatment and the twenty-some pills I now take daily, including heavy narcotics, leaves my bed mattress melting into the forest and desert soils of my love. I lie again on the sandy banks on the Colorado River, a mile deep within Earth's bowels of the Grand Canyon. My privileged seven private rafting trips, rowing my own boat through some of the most challenging whitewater rafting on the planet, gift me with a felt embodiment of deep humility in the face of such power, beauty, and wonder. Hundreds of nights of falling asleep to the narrow serpentine slit of stars overhead at night, rimmed by canyon walls, interspersed with days of being one with Water's flow, leaves me with a sense of surrender into personal power and peace that I would wish for everyone to know.

What I come to know there is that the power of being at one with Water always lies in the moment of Now! It is in the ever-unfolding Now that one reads the current, that one chooses the timing of a stroke, the precise placement of a blade, the amount of strength to apply, and the angle of one's craft in current. And it is in this Now that one holds informing memories and the necessary anticipation of what is to come in the emergence of existence.

My post-diagnosis nights, however, are also filled with the childhood memories of depression, despair, and disempowerment, exacerbated by the writing of this memoir. The fact that our current political environment fills the daily newscasts with stories that awaken and play out the religious childhood traumas of a toxic masculinity, an oppressive God, and a well-meaning abusive father hiding from himself... well, these awaken me with nightmares that haunt my soul and spirit in the Death Lodge too.

Like so many others, I have seen the environmental crisis and cultural wars of our times coming for decades and have felt like a voiceless prophet of darkness screaming into the night. *Now is your time*, I tell myself from within the womb of the Death Lodge. *You were born for this*; I hear as a frequency and vibration coming from the depths of my soul. *Trust yourself. Trust the life-force within. Trust the love of Life seeking expression through you. This is not about you. Be a vessel for what desires to emerge through you. Release attachment to the book's reception. That is not yours to see or own. Just live true to the depths of what you know, Larry. Allow yourself to be simply who you most deeply know your Self to be. Relax into this!*

All this, interspersed with, yes, reminiscent voices repeating, *"You're crazy, Larry!"*

It is from these depths of the Lodge that I feel challenged to clarify how I aspire to meet our paradoxical times, these burning-times eras of accelerating destabilization and chaos as the foundations of the story of separation crumble around us. *That story is trapped in an archetypal fight to the death for its life. It cannot tolerate diversity or equality of rights of existence, having lost reference to Nature's ecological strategies of resilience in turbulent times. Believers seek to make their children and the world into monocultural mirrors of their desired self-image, even as does their god, so cut off from and untrusting of Nature's intelligence are they.*

Opportunistic charlatans proliferate and seek power through feeding off the very fears, anger, and loneliness they nurture. Raging authoritarian would-be strong men will abound, wounded, insecure, and voracious souls they are, compensating through visions of grandeur and greatness. Hiding from their own shadows and divine magnificence, they fail to see or no longer care they serve a concretized self-created idol within, the God of a story of separation and his shadowy needs for superiority that requires inferiors, and affinities for revenge, retribution, death, and destruction.

Meanwhile, the seductive story-powers and software inherent within a literal reading of the Tree of Knowledge of Good and Evil remains unseen by its true believers. Yet it requires of them cancer-like dogmas that proclaim evil is out there, in others, and only themselves and a godly, holy war against evil can save us and our country.

But how do I rightfully respect and honor the Blue Baby, those whose worldviews are so different from my own? What is even mine to own? And how shall I compost what is mine to own into fertile soil for the nurturing of a new yet old and more beautiful story of innate worthiness and belonging?

How do I bring love home, withdraw my righteous projections upon others of their insufficiencies? How do I find the courage to look within for what it is I project outside of this self, and so hate in others?

How do I alchemize and make holy and sacred the potential poisons or medicines of holy rage and grief and sorrow rising so fiercely within, for what is already and will yet be lost of our wild garden planet?

How do I and we boundary those who would control our bodies and lives in their insatiable soul hungers misdirected toward power and profit? Those who charismatically sell snake oil *visions of a return to grandeur to the disillusioned masses for whom the economic and social systems of commodification are an unseen parasite upon their wellbeing?*

These are some of the inquiries the Death Lodge invites of me as I live into the womb of my and our future, whatever it may be.

My system needs vistas and perspectives found in Nature's wilds to help me navigate the political and social challenges of our times. It is during the times of my organizational leadership and development work that I come across the works of Ken Wilber and Barbara Marx Hubbard (Wilber 2007, Hubbard 2020). I am drawn to their focus on the evolution of human consciousness, and particularly to Barbara's wherein she draws on the resources of the inspiring children's book, *Butterfly*, by Norie Huddle (Huddle 1990). Here, Huddle tells of the caterpillar as a voracious hairy worm-of-a-critter (my phrase) whose sole drive in life is growth. It is driven to consume and gorge itself yet endlessly more. Until one day it follows an impulse and finds itself spinning a cocoon of a home, a container of transformational space for the chrysalis to hospice the caterpillar and birth the butterfly.

What comes in the beginning is the molecular dissolution of the caterpillar's body, eyes, skin, intestinal system, and all, into a seemingly disorganized molecular gelatinous goo. The creature's body, however, contains what biologists call *imaginal buds* or cells. These few visionary *seeds* provide an organizing structure within this chrysalis phase to what also seeks to emerge. Interestingly, too, the immune system of the caterpillar attacks the imaginal cells that will give rise to the butterfly (Meade 2024).

But the caterpillar could no more have foreseen itself as a flittering flying creature of migrating beauty, now feeding on and pollinating flowers along its route to a home of ancestral belonging, perhaps thousands of miles away, than I could have forecast the life of beauty and gratitude and wonder and love I now inhabit.

I assert here that this deep ancestral intelligence lives within each of us too. The animating life-force of the universe itself carries this wild wisdom. It is a birthright awaiting the re-memberance of our innate kinship with all life.

And when I/we fall into self-judgments, perfectionism, endless busyness, striving, and us-versus-them thinking, and good-versus-evil mindsets... we are caught in the strategies of the cultural Voracité attacking the imaginal cells of your soul and spirit, belittling you with challenges of, "Who are you to think...?" or "How dare you...!"

And yet without the wild resiliency of the imaginal cells' efforts to organize themselves beyond the familiar and attacking immune system of the old story, the butterfly would never gain the tenacity and strength of wings to fly. So also, for us, it is in the spiraling integration of our struggles, hardships, and joys that we find the gifts of our own soul's path home.

After all, who is the butterfly to get lost in blaming the caterpillar when flower nectars beckon and wind breezes crave the caresses of your wings? Is not the craving for the unbridled "Yes!" to Life the very hunger of our hearts that can guide us into the unfolding more beautiful Now?

This personal learning of our spirits and souls to fly again is a spiraling journey without end, even as is the evolutionary and developmental journey of consciousness. For we each carry the capacities for good and for evil, for creation and for destruction within, and partake of the same with each breath. And to gain the self-authoring discernment of choice as a path is to awaken a spiraling journey into releasing and letting go as much as it is of receiving, for neither the grasping hand, heart, or mind are open. This is a trail of learning to move beyond systemic habituated reactions into the courageous life-claiming ownership of response-ability and personal sovereignty. This is true power. I only find it in the moment-to-moment living of my life.

For to receive the gifts arising from the conscious partaking of the forbidden fruits of the Tree of Life is to incarnate and embody Heaven within. Yes, here on Earth. It is to cease looking outside ourselves for validation of our holy desires, for divinity and its powers, for purpose and meaning, and to look rather within for this birthright of our cosmic origins and belonging.

This is the bringing home of love, so much as I know of it. And I am convinced the greatest offering any of us can bring to the world at this time is that of our own awakening, bringing love home to the wholeness of our ecological selves, our darkness, and our light.

Your Holy Hungers

There is an innate hunger within
It is not meant to sentence you to loneliness
Or curse you with grief, sorrow, depression and despair
Rather it is a gift from the soil and trees and stars
Inviting a deeper listening
A reimagining and reorienting
As to what it even is to be human

For this desire and craving
is like a North Star of the soul
Imprinted in your heart
In-forming your feet and spirit
Of who you most deeply are
So you know where and how to turn
When the need for starting over is greatest

You are wired to orient for connections
The way aspens are one-rooted into their grove
The way the mycelium of mushrooms and fungi
weave a forest floor into a dimensional carpet of interbeing

Belonging is your birthright
You are born out of and into it
Your very being is itself woven of kinship
And now all of Life awaits
This coming home of your spirit to itself
This remembering—
Of our human place within the Family of Life

Like a Butterfly Alighting on Your Heart

We have moved beyond
the horizons where righteous beliefs serve
the truth of who we are
seducing us into illusions
of believing we know where we stand in status
among the swirling of cosmic stars
galore and without end

What might it be instead
to sacrifice upon the Altar of Mystery
the smallness of identities
hinged to superiority or inferiority
separation possessions and achievements
and empty the sacred bowl of self and soul
turn it upside down
let the knowing and answers and false securities fall out
as you assert your willingness to let go
of who they say you are

Drink deep this presence of the Great Unknown
Swim in the wonderment of your very existence
Discover yourself falling utterly in love
just as you are
with what and who
is now right in front of you
and within you
like a butterfly alighting
on the blossoming flower of your heart

The Once and Future Human

If the wandering gray water snake can crawl right out of its own skin
on a summer day along the banks of the Pecos River,

If the singing katydid can shed the confining protection
of its exoskeleton in the juniper tree outside my window,

If the caterpillar in my garden can spin a cocoon and
transmute into a gelatinous goo following some imaginal impulse
into the future of molecular transformation becoming butterfly,

If a raindrop births itself out of ocean
the ocean too can be found in a rain drop
If a bar-tailed godwit can fly seven-thousand miles
from Alaska to New Zealand over open Pacific waters
without stopping or sleeping and no lunch or beverage service—
only a listening
to some internal compass within,

If the one rooted aspen trees in the Sangre de Cristo Mountains
can shed no longer serving leaves—and branches—
growing new limbs and trembling leaves that do,

If the star eyed newborn two-legged girl can carry at birth
within her tiny being the grandmother of generations yet to come—
each and all descendants of a single Mitochondrial Eve
who herself was once a new eyed baby girl,

Who is to say man too cannot be born anew,
twice born now the consciousness within
awakening to itself and the wholeness of Life
realizing the interconnectedness of all that is—
is already vibrant and alive within?

Is this not the story shared
by all the traditions of mystery, wonder and awe—
that this singular self has its inter-being
only within the holy wholeness of—Self?

And that letting go of all one knows
honoring the willingness and courage
to not know—to not name and define at last
to cease reading the maps drawn by those
who live under the spells of answers and knowing
and trust at last...
Oh Yes!

There is already another map within
revealing ecological life-scapes of whitewater rivers
high mountain passes and quiet summer meadows and
vast plains of tall grasses and thirsty desert washes
of dry gravel and of bubbling springs and oasis too...
and a path—

a path known to only the walker
self-revealing only as the pilgrim walks
listening

to the awakening wholeness
that is not his or hers
but lives already within
a potent gift of birthright
awaiting only the opening
the awakening
to the simplest of truths—
to what is

Wild Water's Embrace

Today,
should I wish to change the world,
but one small act is required of me—
challenging though it may in truth be.

For if I wish to ask such vulnerability of others,
my heart, spirit, and soul
must rightfully be willing
to be changed also,
transformed even by that by which
I would change out there, in others.

Thus rises the risk—
the willingness to experience myself differently.
All this requires
is that I have courage enough
to be where
and as I am,
while resting in the embrace of love.

Chapter 12

A MORE BEAUTIFUL NOW

This book is the fulfillment of a promise to my fifteen-year-old self. The promise, as you'll recall, was to write a book tracing my journey, should I ever live life to a place of celebration, so that no other child should have to experience the pain I was in.

Yeah. It was a grandiose dream for anyone, let alone a fifteen-year-old. The story of this book's manifesting could well be another book unto itself. What is here, however, is an attempt to leave cairns, or trail markers traditionally made of stone piles, of turning points and transformational experiences in this journey of my heart.

The prayer is, of course, that there is something useful and inspiring here for others who find themselves living in uncharted realms, and so too with a need for new maps and practices for navigating the edges of chaos and turmoil, of community and personal sovereignty, we collectively face. The vulnerable truth, however, is that I write out of a need to root and integrate the wonderous discoveries of my living, that they may also find their full blossoming in my incarnated heart and living, and in the larger whole.

I've come to see the challenges of integrating altered state experiences as a crucial skill set for the future of our collective thrivability. Our hungers and needs for their gifts of neuroplasticity, creativity, unitary experiences, psychodynamic insights, and more are parallel tracks in our systems, each reflective of the other. Psychedelic mushrooms were likely pivotal in our developmental evolution of mind and consciousness and can again be so in this critical era; Life's love of itself, like water, flows reciprocally throughout a balanced ecosystem between hungers and needs.

My story illustrates the challenging need for integration of even repeated entheogenic encounters with the *divine within*, let alone the singular first one that will likely blow your world apart. The reader is witness to my continuing decades of learning to bring these deep transformational experiences home into natural embodiment. I see the same dynamic in folks who return from profoundly beautiful and transformational wilderness retreats or solo experiences, or from their own altered state psychedelic journeys.

The achieving of such altered states is, in some ways, simplistically stated, the easy part. Rightly held, these sacred altered state rituals and ceremonies begin preparations for the post-journey-high incorporation phase from conception onward. The embodiment of bringing resulting experiences and insights into flourishing identities of wholeness is not something we can achieve alone, however much our domesticated masculine selves might try. For our cultural hyper-individuality is rather the tomb and womb of composting separation's loneliness into the fertile soil-of-community that Charles Eisenstein eloquently writes of in *The More Beautiful World Our Hearts Know is Possible* (Eisenstein 2013).

I desire the personal power to live a story of conscious creation—my "way of looking at and being in the universe,"—one that incarnates sensitivity and a surrender to the flow, balance, and harmony of the Tao. This leaves me living in a landscape of paradoxes, contradictions,

and synchronicities. I live in the shadows and in the light; good and evil entwine within me, as do peace and turbulence. This Mystery is larger than the powers of my light and so intimacy with the forbidden darkness of my personal and our collective unconscious worlds—I seek and practice too. The larger practice here is the willingness and courage to look for what I do not see or know, where my assumptions and presumptions blind me to what is, including to my own shadows. What am I afraid to look at within? I ask of myself. And how do I nourish and sustain the inner wild joys and passions for living that nourish this dance? Surely these are North Stars for living a life of wholeness, of true personal power.

To navigate the cultural loss of reference for wholeness, while living in a world gone mad with the trance of separation, I cultivate practices, rituals, ceremonies, community, and solitude in support of the self I wish to be in this world. This requires daily, and yes, some circumstances require intense moment-to-moment conscious breathing in of the divine deep ecological self that Nature reveals me to be. The seductions into busyness and adrenalized sleepwalking grow yet more powerful with advancing and escalating technologies of distraction, even as our unsustainable consumption reveals a cultural collapse well in process (Bulletin of the Atomic Scientists 2025).

I seek a self that is clear and powerful enough to hold to the truth of my being amidst a challenging collective atmosphere of social disintegration, numbing, denial, and blame-shifting. Such alertness requires me to nurture this container consciously, this self-identity; for I desire to step into the courageous embrace of a love of self that extends even to the disavowed shadows within, and to live thus in the spirit and flow of sufficiency and the gifts of natural abundance our garden planet offers. And while I desire the sacred container of my living to alchemize or boundary out the predators, parasites, and toxicities of the world, I know this is most powerfully done as I choose to focus on and attend to *the more beautiful now* I create through moments of awareness, presence, and choice.

It was a *more beautiful now* moment for me when I met Emmanuel Karisa Baya in 2015, as I arrived at the small conference facility along the Oregon Coast. I'm slowly driving the coastal-green grassy two-track drive to my motel room when I round a corner and encounter a man walking the same path, but towards me. We each stop, perhaps twenty yards apart, and our eyes meet. I see the man standing there just as an enormous, welcoming, open-hearted smile of delight blossoms upon his black face. Immediately, I sense an unusually grounded feeling to his presence. I just know. *This man is deeply rooted into Earth. I feel his feet touch her as he stands there. I want to share time with this man!*

Now, Emmanuel's story of our meeting is different. He claims his smile was so large because he saw something he'd never seen before; "...a tree was driving a car!" That's his story.

We are each there for a retreat hosted by Arnold and Amy Mindell. Arny's book, *The Shaman's Body: A New Shamanism for Transforming Health, Relationships, and the Community* (1993), was a vital confirmation and support for my own journey during challenging times, and I am eager to share the in-person time with him and Amy.

Emmanuel and I arrange for personal time together over lunch, and I learn of his challenging early life in rural Kenya as a child orphaned by nine. He speaks and I feel the child's day-to-day and night-to-night experiences of hunger and thirst, the somatic and emotional tensions of not knowing where or when he might next eat or have water to drink, or a place to sleep. I hear of a passion for learning that drove him, despite the challenges, to finish his primary and secondary schooling and become a certified accountant. His early family roots of farming, however, called him back to his love of intimacy with the land.

He shares the emergence story of the Magarini Children Centre and Organic Demonstration Farm. He speaks of how he began sharing food from his family's field with three children who were too hungry and weak to walk the miles to and from school. A life of synchronicities eventually leads to a scholarship for a year's study of permaculture in Japan with the Asia Rural Institute, and later to becoming an international student and Diplomaed teacher with the Deep Democracy Institute International.

My life walks the tensions between that of the warrior and that of the lover. I find it seductive to fight against and neutralize the power structures of the patriarchal Jehovah Wound. And important as this protective role is, I suspect a devotion to the embodiment of love, in support of visionary expressions of *a more beautiful now*, is what will inspire and sustain our spirits through these chrysalis times. Emmanuel clearly lives into a vision of the latter, and I instinctively desire to support him and his work. We are like two drops of water who recognize also the ocean in the drop of the other.

Thus, my involvement with Emmanuel and the Centre begins when there were around one hundred children there. Now, as I write, nearly four hundred children, boys and girls, are fed and educated, and roughly half are also housed there.

Their education is holistic, incorporating evening fires and wisdom-storytelling with community elders, for example, and goes beyond the formal government curriculum in other areas as well. The children learn self-care and reliance as they practice the skills of regenerative farming and the grounding philosophy of what Emmanuel calls, *Peace from the Soil.* "If we love the soil, it loves us back and teaches us to love ourselves and each other," he says (Baya 2020).

And as the children experientially learn the self is an ecological one that grows out of interdependency and inter-breathing, they learn to talk with, to listen, and be present to, the trees in the food forest they plant with their hands and whom they sit with as friends and give water and names to. With their hands in the dirt, they learn to be present with the soil and sense it speak of its health and needs. The crops of peas and maize and more speak too, and the children learn the needs of these green ones as well, like which plants like to be in community near each other, and how to catch and conserve rainwater through swells and contours and ponds upon the land. Through this, they also learn the skills of self-care and love, community and peacemaking as skills of social and emotional intelligence and to fertilize and embody the soil and water—as teacher, healer, and lover. "To love the soil is to love yourself," Emmanuel says simply.

"We are having a bad drought," he tells me over lunch. "The traditional rains have not come. We travel eighteen miles to fill our jerry cans with water... and then we share this with the plants. The climate patterns are not what they used to be, and we can no longer count on the rains to be there for planting our crops. We need to drill a well but—"

It will be four years before that well is drilled and I am simultaneously blessed to visit Emmanuel at the Centre. There, I delight in the wild joys of drums gifting rhythm to my dancing barefoot on the mother soil of our collective and my personal African one-rooted ancestry, genetically traced back to the Mitochondrial Eve. I like to imagine she too danced to the drumming of her heart with the naked soles of her feet, some one hundred and fifty-five thousand years ago,

"I've never seen such poverty before, or such richness of the human spirit," I repeatedly hear from visitors to the Centre. Located in Kilifi County, the remote and rural area of the Centre is indeed one of extreme poverty. And the notable richness of spirit there is exemplified by this story from Emmanuel, told during one of the recent extreme water shortages. "The children sit together in groups of four to six and share a glass of water."

Each child savors a sip and then passes this elixir of life on to the next child. My imagination tells me every sip is treasured slowly.

This island of connectivity that the Centre represents for me is a complete worldview turnaround from the *Lord of the Flies* (Golding 1954), *Nineteen Eighty-Four* (Orwell 1949), or *Brave New World* (Huxley 1932), predictive dystopian influencing novels of my youth. Learning to listen to the soil, plants, and trees teaches the children to listen also to the world with their hearts and hands and minds. This teaches them principles of mutualism, symbiosis and reciprocity, predators and prey, boundary setting, and the values of self-initiative and communal vision and cooperation. And the Magarini Centre is but one of uncountable regenerative seeds nurturing an indigenous vision and flourishing love of life that can be the future we choose.

I find inspiration in such young hearts knowing they are in the hard and the good times together, interdependently, and co-creatively with the water and soil, sun and air, seeds and trees, chickens and pigs, and honeybees and butterflies too. They inspire me to cultivate practices for re-membering the same, and for the cultivation of intentional communities that are possible as we reweave wholeness back into the story of who we are.

One such gratitude and abundance practice for me is to sip from my first glass of water in the mornings with simple mindfulness and gratitude. In this ritual, I open my heart to the One Water that greens and gives life to this planet—Gaia.

With this sip, my spirit drinks deeply from the mystical Waters of Life and is simultaneously connected through the physical water from my faucet to all the waters of the world, whether they float in the sky or on Earth's skin or in subterranean veins within her body. Gratitude for the wealth of this water in my life connects me to the blood of my flesh, to all flesh, layered geological histories of oceans, forests, deserts, and stone, and to all those who take such wealth for granted, and to those growing numbers who live in thirst.

The words *metacrisis* and *polycrisis* grow in usage even as their impacts converge, entwine, and complexify in our age of misinformation and disinformation amplified by social media algorithms and artificial intelligence. Jonathan Gustin, of the Purpose Guides Institute (purposeguides.org), introduced me to the thinking that the metacrisis is rooted in the story of identity, the worldview or paradigm we bring to the circumstance. It is the story as seen from the "I" within the story. The polycrisis is the outer manifestation of our accumulative loss of reference to Earth's natural systems, the consequences of our story of separation coming home.

This is an attempt to language the reality of the cobweb of intermingling crises we face. We cannot separate migration issues, climate disruption, economic challenges, housing shortages, resource depletion, polarizations of politics and religion, increasing trends of loneliness and depression, declines in church attendance, addictions, homelessness, poverty, school shootings (polycrisis) from the personal and collective stories of identity we live, that no longer serve (metacrisis).

We face not problems that can be solved, but entangled conundrums which are beyond solving by the minds of their creators. The evolutionary deep invitation here is to find ways to live into these challenges that allow a gathering of the collective intelligence and wisdom residing in the innate inheritance of our belonging to the sacred circle of life. As we awaken, this will require the hospice of confronting and integrating our personal and collective griefs and sorrows and sacred rage for the world now dying. *The Work that Reconnects* (workthatreconnects.org), developed by Joanna Macy and expressed at School for The Great Turning (schoolforthegreatturning.com), is one pioneering resource in this field.

Cosmologist and historian Thomas Berry, in his visionary book, *The Great Work*, summarizes the challenge of releasing the old story even as we live into the new and emerging story of our innate belonging thusly: "Our greatest single need is to accept this story of the universe, as we now know it as our sacred story. It could be considered the most magnificent of all creation stories." (Berry 1999, 83)

My first exciting assignment with the Mountain Center, after closing the Lookout at the end of the fire season in 1983, was to drive a van full of resupply food and water for a couple of juvenile delinquent groups on their fifteen-day Wilderness Experience programs. It was solo time again for me and I'd never been to the remote Burr desert country of Utah and getting paid to camp out *in the middle of nowhere* by myself for five days, sleeping out in the open on the ground and under mesmerizing stars—I mean, how good can life get?

My manuscript from the Lookout of perhaps thirty typed pages was secured with a paperclip in a common tan manila folder. I confess to feeling self-righteously proud as I prepared to unveil the Jehovah of my youth to the world with the publication of the paper. But for five days it was windy, rainy, and cool. So much for my naïve dream of desert-hanging and editing while sitting comfortably on the ground with a warm sun for comfort.

Then on about day three the wind stopped, and the sun came out. So did I, with my tarp on the ground and manuscript beside me now in a loose pile. Feeling self-satisfied, I closed my eyes to meditate and enjoy the sun's warmth and the wind's stillness.

A whirling dervish whirlwind from Hell, as I felt it, came out of nowhere in a flash. Just as quickly, the only copy of my summer's worth of writing was aswirl all around me as pages took wings amidst the blinding, blowing sand. I watched them gain elevation in a rising and widening spiral that eventually took the whole holy lot of them out of sight overhead—just disappeared, along with my dreams.

I didn't write again for two years. Not a journal entry. Not a poem. Who could I tell such a story to? And why would I? It was all just too much of a mystery to me. And so unfair of the universe, to steal this life purpose from me.

But here you are now, holding the landing of that whirlwind's energy in your hands. Or perhaps you're listening to it through an audio version. And we pass each other in the grocery store aisles or as in my dream, together we sit at a round table and one by one begin to look each other in the eyes and assert, "You know what? I think I'm awake and dreaming a story too!"

And slowly, the dream stories are shared and together we listen and help each other awaken to the skills of living into a *more beautiful now*. Together we learn to come to nature as teacher, healer, and lover, inspired and informed by her as we compost the legacies of domination and control meta-stories into good soil for the emergence of *a new earth*, a new era of co-creative dreaming into and manifesting our sacred kinship with all of life.

Together we sit at the table of our dreams and remember that to love thy neighbor of fur, fin, wing, scale or bark, or of two legs… is to love thyself, for the two and multitudes are one, even as the aspen grove arises from one root.

The alchemized spiritual core and essence of what the mushrooms repeatedly reveal to me through the decades is a three-fold vision. First is the inner, underlying unity of all things.

Second is the taproot of evil lives in meta-stories that withdraw recognition of this divine unity, or sacredness, from any part of oneself, or from another. Wherever I/we do not bring love to ourselves, I/we embody the Jehovah Wound. We deny ourselves Heaven on Earth and become self-perpetrators, servants, and victims to the original heresy, the stories of insufficiency and unworthiness, all fruits of the mythological tree of knowledge of good and evil.

Last, the cosmos itself, and thus we humans too, are so much grander than our day-to-day cultural living allows for the exploration and appreciation of.

In the light of such fungal revelations, is the cultural suppression of entheogenic soul medicine any wonder? And no wonder, too, the rush by the powers of separation and division to privatize and commodify, without regard for social costs, Nature's wild wonders of old-growth forests, wild waters, and dark emerald studded skies that can bring a human soul to its knees in awe of such feral beauty. People who come to know such beauty and magnificence as the landscape of their own inner being are not ones to bow before human constructions of authoritarian, fascist, or oligarchic regimes. We are guided rather by visions of a more beautiful story, *a more beautiful Now*, for we know what true power is, and where it lives.

Yes, *Now* is the time for the collective awakening to the powers of our wild divine heritage. Let us hold hands as we walk into these unknown times, for there is a map in our hearts that knows the way. The spark of divinity we each carry brightens the way for all. And as this cosmic fire of our belonging awakens, so too does the water within us, the very Waters of Life that know how to flow, how to embrace what is, and so cut through the rigidities of solid rock and politicized agendas of religious division and control.

These are the same hydraulics that allow the dandelion seed to germinate below the surface of black-asphalt pavement, and to find its way up through the micro-cracks of overlay and then to blossom into yellow beauty. And so too the seeds of love and of Earth awakening to herself spread.

Earth and all her children await our choosing the telling of, and living into, this ancient story born anew. Even our ancestors pray, "May these be the ones who release the traumas of history and open their minds and hearts and so bring love home to the wholeness of their being. We await your healing, so we, too, may be healed."

Blessings on your journey home, dear readers, friends, family, and fellow travelers all. Wild joys await.

On Not Knowing

I do not know how
to be in this world
of such grand beauty

Red Tail Hawk circles overhead
caresses with love the currents of wind
Golden Ponderosa Pine tree trunks soar
and tower above me too
as their crowns blow and dance

While the soil of their rooting and under my soles
is denser with DNA
than the brain tissues in my skull

Oh I can go on endlessly with such
celebrations and wonders of life embracing itself
as a butterfly now alights on my hand

But the sorrows of our world are great too
and seemingly as endless
as a bespeckled sky of stars glistening
on a dark new moon night

Life's great extinctional die-off of human times
arises now out of a seductive story
of humanity's superiority and embedded tales
of separation from and dominion over all non-human kindred

But there is another story
alive and well within me
My own intimate drinking
of the Waters of Life
quench the innate thirst for belonging
leave me satiated
with gratitude wonderment and awe
for this gift of breath
shared by all my kin

And so I long that you too
might know such wild joys
like that awakening
of the Spirit of Love within
that leaves me not knowing
how to live in this world
but to love it

Alchemies of Grief and Sorrow

Oh the wild joys of my grief
are heavy upon me this morning
though in truth
they are never far
from my awareness these days
for there is much grieving
desperate to be allowed room to roam
within the landscapes of my life and
seeking to inform my attention and days and living

for the coming poverty of the world
is great without the 120-million-year-old sea turtles
and their wondrous migrations of rebirth
and without the marvelous dancing honeybees
pollinating our imaginations and food
where and how will we humans live
if we do not re-member our inter-breathing with all of Life

how will the trees migrate
and where will all the people go
who lose homes to the rise of sea waters
climatic mega-droughts that leave mouths too dry for speech
hungry stomachs that cannot wait
and how easy it is to fight for scarce resources
rather than to live courageously
into the vulnerable inter-relatedness of our being

oh but the alchemies of allowing
such grief and sorrow into my spirit and soul
is indeed transformational and so also wild
for in this I am changed
transmuted even and now know this body
of you and I and we and they
us and them of skin and scale and feather
we are but One
in the end

and in this awareness rises an ecological comfort
that even unspeakable rage pain and suffering
held within the sacred circle of belonging
carry a medicine of inexplicable transformative joy
married to my grief and sorrow

When Trees Say Yes

I fell in love with a tree today.
Proposed, I did.

She said, "Yes, but...
only if you embrace and entwine our roots
and thus truly inhabit and live equally
in the underworld with me too."

The trees, they do talk, you know.
And today I discovered
they are generous with their love too.
For as rumors spread of our betrothal,
others quickly begin to present themselves,
and to ask, "But what of me?"
Soon there is a chorus throughout the whole of forest.
Wherever I walk or look, I hear,
"But what of me?"

They each sing,
in a song of their own,
"Am I not beautiful too?"

They conspire and release their delicious intoxications.
Scents of various pines and aspens and oaks
of soil and lichens and rocks too envelope me
and I cannot help but inspire
their very being into mine.

My soul recognizes this conscious inter-breathing
as a transformation of the familiar self
I know as home.
Fear for the loss of my human identity does arise.

Yet what, pray tell, is a real man to do?
I say, "Yes!" of course,
to the whole holy lot of 'em.

And now, pray tell me true:
What is a man
if he be not a tree,
and even a forest too?

One People

That I am enough
Oh to feel such a sufficiency of being in the world
Oh to belong with an innate intimacy
to rest in the birthright
of emergence from the womb
with indigenous worth and identity
to receive and to know
through a primal intelligence and wisdom alive within
one's place in the world
is held in a sacred circle of community
a landscape of relationships and story
ecologically interwoven of with all of Life

I and you and we and they
all born into kinship
Earthlings all
invited into openness marvel wonder and delight
as we swim together in awareness and gratitude
for the great unspeakable mystery
in which we find ourselves
Awakening
and enough
just as we are

I Am a Child of You, Stars, and Sun

of you, Fire, spark and flame of my life
in every cell of my body
That I Am

I am a child of you, Water,
of your drops and flakes, rivers, oceans and fluidly flowing clouds
in every cell of my body
That I Am

I am a child of you, Air,
of your unseen yet felt and vital energizing presence
in every cell of my body
That I Am

I am a child of you, Soil,
informer of digestion, integration, releasing and gifting back
in every cell of my body
That I Am

I am a child of you, Earth,
wondrous Mother of my own rooting into this life
in every cell of my body
That I Am

I am a child of you, Moon,
of your cycles of birthing into death and rebirth
in every cell of my body
That I Am

I am a child of you, oh unspeakable Mystery,
      weaver of Life's polarities into the wholeness of One
          in every aspect of my being
             That I Am

             Thank you
             I honor you
             I love you

Appendix

LIST OF POEMS

The poems herein are intended to carry the energetics of the book but through poetic induction, in contrast to prosaic rationality. For the reader's ease of reference, they are listed here with page numbers. For the gift of a free e-book download of these poems, please go to larryglover.com/WJbookpoetry.

ACKNOWLEDGMENTS

I've spent a lot of my life living with the self-image of *the lone cowboy*. From the perspective of *now*, however, reality reveals itself to be far different from that of the solo John Wayne masculine image I learned to cultivate. The blessed truth is that my life is an ecological weaving of a wealth of relationships.

Neither I, nor this book, would exist without the invitational frustrations and challenges gifted me by some, and certainly not without the support and encouragement and simple presence of so many others. A book that is nearly sixty years in the writing, amidst the walking of many professional paths, accumulates uncountable gifts of gratitude.

My life and this book are shaped by many fellow travelers including during my time at a shelter for runaway youth in inner-city Detroit, the Payette National Forest Service in Idaho, my Santa Fe Mountain Center days, by time spent in experiential organizational leadership and high-performance training and development, and of course, by fifty contiguous years providing various nature-based retreat programs.

And all of you uncountable friends and colleagues, who, over the decades, read manuscripts and offered emotional support in service of "Larry's writing a book..." Thank you!

To my brothers, Benny, Mickey, and Joe. I would not be whom I am without you. You are each a special inspiration and blessing in my life, and I am proud of you. To my deceased sister Kay, through your spirits of perseverance, tenacity, and laughter, you endured hardships beyond naming from an early age and so became a model for me when I most needed these attributes.

Mom and Dad, I am grateful for your gift of Life to me. Thank you for inviting me into this walking and breathing eco/mytho/poetic mystery of self-creation we each are. I am now also grateful for the gifts delivered within the sacred container of wounding, through your own unhealed traumas, ones inevitably delivered through your parenthood.

That I inherited your love of nature's beauty, Mother, of sunrises and sunsets, is a life-sustaining gift to me. Dad, that you were ashamed of my pride and spirit, that your "spare the rod and spoil the child" theology gifted me with a hatred of you and God and hypocrisy, alchemically gifted me with a love of truth and the life-transforming discovery of a shadow-self living within.

That your combined wills to dominate and make me into the image of a person you believed a Church of Christ preacher's son should be, that you tried to make your children into "the world's best Christians," offered me opportunities to learn to choose loyalties to a truth of wholeness-of-Self over loyalties to theology, dogma, and tradition. Thank you.

You initiated me into a story of manhood as you received and knew it and into the delusional Truth(s) of black-and-white thinking. That you valued loyalty to Faith over the hard science of fossils held in my hand, that you feared my receiving an education beyond the Biblically ordained one as you understood it, that you inseminated me with shame for my existence and a theology of never enough-ness, and so gave me something concrete and worth rebelling against, thank you.

Without such unconscious gifts, I might never have been desperate enough to set off into the forbidden and uncharted waters of self-discovery and of throwing away an inherited map of reality.

To the Lord Jehovah, God the Father, of my youth, thank you for teaching me to honor the Trickster Shadow living within and without, and for a literacy of the power of story to shape the life I choose to live. And yes, one intention within this book is to name and call out your shadow energetics.

To those whom I wounded along the way of my journey into greater healing and wholeness, I am sorry for my lapses of integrity, for whatever wounding I perpetuated. I pray you find the gift of your way into forgiveness, even as I am learning to bring love home.

Thank you to the thousands of clients over the decades—from those some might label as "juvenile delinquents" to the adult "criminally insane," as well as sexual victims, pedophile priests, and mental health practitioners learning the ropes of experiential therapy, to wilderness therapists enhancing their nature-based skills for self-care. To those from the government, from international business communities, and those courageous and often desperate souls joining me for wild journeys of day hikes to multi-day wilderness retreats and solo quests—thank you, all. You inspire me.

To my traditional Northern Cheyenne brother, Billford Curley Senior, who never ceases from his prayers for the completion of this book, nor from his dedication to the children, "so they may know where they came from and who they are." To Emmanuel Karisa Baya and Jescar Mubuche, co-founders of the Magarini Children Centre and Organic Farming Demonstration Farm, my Kenyan brother and sister of shared ancestral rooting, for creating and modeling an inspiring community rooted into Earth as a source and model for attunement and harmony with self and others, thank you.

To my Spirit Animal Allies:
- Bear for saving my life and initiating me into breath,
- Eagle for teaching me the value of vast vision,
- Owl for teaching me to see and listen into and befriend the realms of shadow and darkness,
- Serpent for initiating me into the cycles of death and rebirth.

To the directions in the Sacred Circle of Life:
- NE for teaching me to attend to what is seeking birth,
- SE for teaching me to notice what is hungering to grow,
- SW for teaching me the value of focusing my attention on nurturing that which I would harvest and for letting go of the rest,
- NW for teaching me gratitude for the harvest in preparation for resting in the womb of stillness and silence.

To the Elementals:
- Fire for teaching me about passion and transformation,
- Water for teaching me of flow and letting go,
- Air for teaching me of the invisible worlds of Spirit,
- Earth for teaching me about rooting and belonging.

Cheryl Slover-Linett (leadfeather.org), this book would not exist but for your encouragement and believing in me. For over a decade now, you have been the best of business partners and a colleague in conscious personal, spiritual, and professional development and excellence. Your invaluable friendship lives in the heart of my heart.

To my life partner and love, fellow adventurer and explorer of all places wild, Dorothy Beatty, your nurturing support and presence, despite "the madness of my writing," spans decades...

and is fundamentally supportive of me simply being me. No gift is greater, and my gratitude is unmeasurable.

Finally, to Christine Kloser and the team at Seshat Press, thank you. Your patience and guidance provided the sacred container required for the manifesting of this book into print. Thank you.

RESOURCES

Please visit larryglover.com for free gifts, resource support, and contact information.

REFERENCES

Barton, Bruce. 1925. *The Man Nobody Knows*. Bobbs-Merrill Company

Bateson, Gregory. 1972. *Steps to an Ecology of Mind*. Balantine Books

Baya, Emmanuel Karisa. 2020. "Peace from the Soil." Wild Resiliency Awakening. February 7th, 2020. https://wildresiliency.com/peace-from-the-soil/

Berry, Thomas. 1999. *The Great Work: Our Way Into the Future*. Bell Tower

Bulletin of the Atomic Scientists, 2025. "It Is Now 89 Seconds To Midnight." January 28th, 2025. https://thebulletin.org/doomsday-clock/

Catton, William R. 1982. Overshoot: *The Ecological Basis of Revolutionary Change*. University of Illinois Press

Campbell, Joseph. 1991. *A Joseph Campbell Companion: Reflections on the Art of Living*. HarperCollins

Castaneda, Carlos. 1993. *The Art of Dreaming*. HarperCollins

Comfort, Alex, 1972. The Joy of Sex. Crown Publishing Group

Eisentein, Charles. 2013. *The More Beautiful World Our Hearts Know is Possible*. North Atlantic Books

Golding, William, 1954. *Lord of the Flies*. Faber & Faber

Hall, Edward T. 1959. *The Silent Language*. Doubleday

Hesse, Hermann. 2008. *Siddhartha*. Translated Susan Bernofsky. New York. Modern Library

Hoffer, Eric. 1951. *The True Believer: Thoughts on the Nature of Mass Movements*. New York. Harper & Row

Hubbard, Barbara Marx. 2020. Foundation for Conscious Evolution. https://www.barbaramarxhubbard.com

Huddle, Norie. 1990. *Butterfly*. New York. Huddle Books

Huxley, Aldous. 1932. *Brave New World*. Chatto & Windus

Huxley, Aldous. 1954. *The Doors of Perception And Heaven and Hell*. New York. HarperPerennial

Jung, C.G. and Aniela Jaffé. 1963. *Memories, Dreams, Reflections*. Pantheon Books

Kazantzakis, Nikos. 1955. *The Last Temptation of Christ*. Simon & Schuster

Lamb, F Bruce. 1971. *Wizard of the Upper Amazon: The Story of Manuel Córdova-Rios*. Berkeley. North Atlantic Books.

Macy, Joanna Macy, School for the Great Turning, https://schoolforthegreatturning.com

Mattison, Mark M. *The Gospel of Thomas: A Public Domain Translation*. https://www.academia.edu/15107954/The_Gospel_of_Thomas_A_Public_Domain_Translation

Meade, Michael. 2024. "Why We Resist Change." Living Myth, September 18. Podcast, 30:00. https://www.mosaicvoices.org/episode-401-why-we-resist-change

McKenna, Terence. 1993. *Food of the Gods: The Search for the Original Tree of Knowledge: A Radical History of Plants, Drugs and Human Evolution*. Bantam

Mindell, Arnold. 1993. *The Shaman's Body: A New Shamanism for Transforming Health, Relationships, and the Community*. HarperOne

Moali, Dr Nazanin. 2023. "How To Experience Your First Breath Orgasm with Anya Laeta." Podcast. February 14th. https://sexologypodcast.com/2023/02/14/how-to-experience-your-first-breath-orgasm-with-anya-laeta/

Mowat, Farley. 1963. *Never Cry Wolf*. Toronto. McClelland and Stewart

Neihardt, John G. 1961. *Black Elk Speaks: Being a Holy Man of the Oglala Sioux*. Lincoln. University of Nebraska Press

Nin, Anaïs, 1966. *The Diary of Anais Nin.* Swallow Press

Orwell, George. 1949. *Nineteen Eighty-Four*. Secker and Warburg

Pagels, Elaine. 2004. *Beyond Belief: The Secret Gospel of Thomas*. Vintage.

Plath, Sylvia, 1962. *The Bell Jar*. Harper and Row

Rohr, Richard. 2019. *The Universal Christ: How a Forgotten Reality Can Change Everything We See, Hope For, and Believe*. Convergent Books.

Sahtouris, Elisabet. 2000. *Earth Dance: Living Systems in Evolution.* iUniversity Press

Schultes, Richard Evans and Hofmann, Albert. 1979. *Plants of the Gods: Their Sacred, Healing, and Hallucinogenic Powers* Rochester. Healing Arts Press.

Tsu, Lao, 1972. *Tao Te Ching.* Translated by Gia-Fu Feng and Jane English. Vintage Books.

Wheatley, Margaret J and Myron Kellner-Rogers. 1996. *A Simpler Way.* San Francisco. Berrett-Koehler Publishers Inc.

Wilber, Ken. 2007. *Up from Eden: A Transpersonal View of Human Evolution.* Quest Books

ABOUT THE AUTHOR

A challenging childhood, which included suicidal ideations by the age of nine, gifted Larry with the experience of turning to nature for solace and learning. These rough years found him giving his life to God and becoming a young preacher man before losing his faith and becoming an outcast from his former fundamentalist religious community, preacher father, and mother.

The path of his awakening to the wholeness of Self found him selling his blood for food money, spending his last quarter for a cup of Spokane's black coffee on a winter's morning, and digging for food out of a Safeway dumpster. He once walked into the wilds to die—or to come out a different man—and Larry credits a black bear he met at the door of his tent, nostrils to nostrils, with saving his life.

Larry has worked as a family therapist, social science research consultant, initial attack forest firefighter, fire lookout, wilderness therapist and guide, and internationally as a coach for high-performance leadership and teamwork.

Larry's work, through The Wild Resiliency Network, and in partnership with the non-profit Lead Feather, represents the coalescing of his diverse background and interests in an ecological model of human change and transformation. His work and life are informed and inspired by Indigenous wisdom and Western living systems thinking, quantum and complexity sciences, the emerging science of resiliency, the fields of deep and of spiritual ecology, the junctures of depth, eco- and terra-psychology, and by world mythologies. And of course, through decades of engagement with psychedelic plant medicines.

Please visit larryglover.com for free gifts, resource support, and contact information.

www.ingramcontent.com/pod-product-compliance
Lightning Source LLC
Chambersburg PA
CBHW070548130626
46556CB00001B/72